Sensual Astrology for the African American Woman

Everything You Need to Know About Your Man Through His Sun Sian.

Sensual Astrology for the African American Woman

Everything You Need to Know About Your Man Through His Sun Sign.

S.R. Covington

URBAN *Renaissance*

www.urbanbooks.net

Urban Books, LLC
78 East Industry Court
Deer Park, NY 11729

Sensual Astrology for the African American
Woman Copyright © 2008 S.R. Covington

ISBN 13: 978-1-60162-321-8
ISBN 10: 1-60162-321-6

First Mass Market Printing October 2011
First Trade Paperback Printing May 2008
Printed in the United States of America

10 9 8 7 6 5 4 3 2 1

Distributed by Kensington Publishing Corp.
Submit Wholesale Orders to:
Kensington Publishing Corp.
C/O Penguin Group (USA) Inc.
Attention: Order Processing
405 Murray Hill Parkway
East Rutherford, NJ 07073-2316
Phone: 1-800-526-0275
Fax: 1-800-227-9604

Introduction

Have you ever looked at a couple that's been together forever and wondered how they do it? Or maybe you are the single sister who can't figure out why every guy you meet seems to end up cheating on you. Then again, maybe you've been on a few dates with a man and he seems great, but you want to know if there's potential for anything long-term. Well, believe it or not, the answers to all of these dilemmas might lie in the sun signs of the people involved.

The couple that's celebrating their fiftieth wedding anniversary might be a Taurus man and a Cancer woman. Their union works because both signs are homebodies and crave the same kind of connection. Now, if the man had married a strong-willed Leo woman, they might have been in divorce court long before the fiftieth. As for the single sister who keeps choosing cheating mates, if she would just stop dating Gemini men and find a more faithful sign, she might have better luck with her relationships. And yes, you can get an idea of your long-term possibilities with that new man once you know if his sun sign is compatible with yours.

This is where *Sensual Astrology for the African American Woman* comes in. This book will help you understand the brothers in your life—their behavior, their personality traits, their likes and dislikes, and the truth about their relationship potential. *Sensual Astrology for the African American Woman* describes in detail your most compatible mate. It'll help you choose Mr. Right or Mr. Right Now, depending on where you're hanging out and what you're looking for. If you're looking for your soul mate, well, this book will help you learn why some men are better qualified for that job than others. On the other hand, if you are a sister who likes to play with fire for the sheer thrill of getting burned, then this book will lead you to the brother who'll take you straight into the flames.

Whether you've been with the same man for years or he's someone you just met last week, let's admit that we could all use a little help understanding our men. That's why you should find out his sign and start with the section that will give you a complete rundown on the brother in question. If he's a Leo, then turn to YOUR LEO MAN, and read all about the sign with the over-sized ego and the heart of gold. This is the place where you'll get an explanation for why your Leo always wants to be the center of attention, and why he always has to be right. You'll also be reminded of his incredible generosity. This section will teach you about the behavior you can expect from the Lion, and perhaps you'll gain a few pointers on how to tame the king of the jungle.

Now, if you've set your sights on someone but he hasn't asked you out on that first date yet, then you should move on to the next section, titled LET'S GET IT STARTED. This is where you'll gain insights into each sign's likes and dislikes and find out how to attract his attention. You might think, don't I just have to look cute and flirt a little? But it's not that simple. Think of it like going into Starbuck's. Sure, every man in the line likes coffee, but they won't all order it the same way. The Aries man will be intrigued by the woman in the tight-fitting dress who showers him with compliments all night long. The Virgo man, however, is looking for a smart woman who will stimulate his mind just as much as his body.

Once you've gotten his attention and things are moving in the right direction between you two, then it's time to take it to that next step—

into the bedroom. Again, this book has just the help you need in that department. Turn to the section titled SEX and you'll learn about how these brothers hold it down in the bedroom, and what they'll want from you.

Now, not all of them are going to want it the same way or have the same sexual fantasies, and lucky for you it's been narrowed down by sun signs in this book. While the Scorpio likes a woman with some experience, if it's a young Cancer man you plan to get busy with, you might want to wear that virgin white because of his fragile ego. If it's a Taurus you've been stalking, well, he won't really care if he's your first or you have the experience of Superhead, as long as you keep your attention on him and sing his praises all night long. But whatever sign your man is, you can be sure he'll thank you for reading this section and learning how to turn him on.

If, even with all the great sex, you've decided to end your relationship, there's help for that too. Flip on over to the section titled MOVING ON WITHOUT DRAMA to find out how to leave a particular sun sign without all the usual head-aches—or, in some cases, the knock-down drag-out fights. Let's say you've had all the clinginess you can take from your romantic Pisces and you want out, but the brother is so darn charming he keeps pulling you back in. Well, this section will offer some surefire ways to convince the sensitive Fish that it's time for him to move on. Using the advice in this section, you can even extract yourself from the possessive Aries without provoking his rage.

When you've had enough time to get over your breakup, of course you'll be looking for a new man, right? Well, that's what the section titled COMPATIBILITY is there for. Before you start dating again, check out the men's signs and read up on which ones will be most compatible with yours. That way, when your coworker insists on setting you up on a blind date with her Sagittarius cousin, you'll know before you ever meet him whether your signs hold any long-term possibilities. And if you're visiting match.com and getting more offers than you can handle, checking out each sign's compatibility with yours will definitely help you narrow down your list of possibilities.

Sure, we all know that astrology isn't an exact science. And when it comes to finding your perfect mate, there's no denying that little thing called chemistry, no matter what the man's sign is. Every once in a while you'll meet a couple whose zodiac signs say they should have been nothing but a one-night stand, yet they've been happily married for years. They've got some kind of attraction or bond that no manual could ever describe. But for those of us who'd like a little help in understanding that complex being that is the African American man, this book can be a good starting point. Use it as a tool to guide you in finding a man, or to help you navigate the relationship you're already in. Go ahead and have fun with it. Who knows? You might just find your perfect mate.

Aries
March 21–April 19

Your Aries Man

Did you just run into a man with a tight physique and an upbeat personality? You can be sure he's an Aries man. But before you jump to get his attention, let me give you the rundown on the Aries.

Being the first sign of the Zodiac, Aries represents birth. Like a child, the Aries man relates to the world in the same way that it relates to him. This means that if you're fun and easygoing, that's the Aries you'll get; but if you're uptight and angry, well then, that's the Ram you'll most likely come home to. But whichever Aries you get, you are sure to get one who wants to feel like he's in control. If you're the independent type of woman who can handle her life just fine without the assistance of a male, don't even bother with the Ram. He needs to feel valuable to the woman in his life.

Of course, there can be some benefits to a relationship with him. Aries is the type who loves to be a gentleman. He prefers it when he's taking care of you, so any opportunity he can get to be chivalrous will make him happy. Don't rush to open your own car door. Let him open it for you, and enjoy yourself as he takes you by the hand to escort you into the restaurant, where he is likely to pick up the bill. He will enjoy treating you like his special woman.

Part of this special treatment might include some nice jewelry or a few new designer outfits. Aries is a go-getter when it comes to making money. Most likely he will be an entrepreneur. He has a determination to succeed, and often this means his pockets are fat and he's willing to share with you. But beware: although money is important, it's not always a priority. Aries may not be a good money manager, so there might be times when his wallet is a little light. If you're willing to ride the wave with him, you might be rewarded with a few great shopping sprees when his money is flowing again.

If you desire these types of perks, though, be prepared to play the submissive role in order to keep the peace in a relationship with an Aries man. A friend who was in a long-term relationship with an Aries man, said he once told her, "Look, both of us can't wear the pants in this relationship."

You might find it a challenge to disagree with an Aries man, especially when he's passionate about a particular subject. He has no problem voicing his opinion, but when you disagree, you run the risk of bruising his very fragile ego. You have to be more Southern belle than hood rat when you state your opinions. And when he needs you to listen, make sure you're ready to give him your full attention—no matter what time of the day or night. The Aries male is quite ambitious, hardworking and aggressive. If he needs to get something off his mind, he sees nothing wrong with waking you at 3:00 A.M. to discuss it. As far as he's concerned, why shouldn't you wake up to hear him out? After all, he's awake. That's all that matters.

No matter how much you want to strangle him for waking you out of a really good dream, don't dismiss his feelings. As a partner, he can be quite bossy and dominant, but also warm, caring and affectionate. Remind yourself of all the kind, wonderful things he's done for you then listen patiently. Cuddle up next to him and tell him how great he is to soothe his li'l ole ego, and everyone will get a good night's sleep.

After you've gotten enough rest, be prepared to be on the go. Aries is attracted to a woman who can keep up with him athletically as well as sexually. He is spontaneous, so it's a good idea to have your Nikes packed because he can easily go from rock-climbing to parasailing while most people are just waking up. If you possess a bold, adventurous side and never worry about breaking your newly manicured fingernails, then this might be the man for you.

The biggest problem with the Aries's need for stimulation and excitement is that sometimes he can't help hanging at the club to find it. His ego requires that he get plenty of attention all the time—from all kinds of admirers. If you're looking to settle down, you might want to wait until he's a bit older. Don't go into the relationship thinking he's going to be a one-woman kind of man, at least not in the beginning. Faithfulness won't come until later in the Ram's life.

If you have the energy to handle an active, sexy man with an occasional wandering eye, then get to work on winning the heart of an Aries man. For the woman willing to work with his faults and stroke his ego, the rewards can be great. He'll make you feel like the most special woman in the world, both in and out of the bedroom.

Let's Get It Started

This strong, fit man likes to hang with a partner he feels is all woman. If you want to catch his eye, slither out of a red sports car (red is one of the Aries male's favorite colors) with a pair of high stilettos and a dress that clings to you in all the right places. Glance at him as you pass by, but don't linger. It's important to let him know you're interested, as long as you don't take the lead. That's his job.

Remember: as good as you might look in that dress, you do not want him to catch you eyeing the other brothers as you make your way into the club. That alone will turn this Aries man off. See, he doesn't mind the chase, as long as he knows you're interested in him, and only him.

Once you're in the club, if he approaches you, this is a great sign! You have captured his attention, so you can be sure you're everything he wants in a female. Aries doesn't waste time on anything he considers second best.

Now that he's made the first move, tread carefully with this man and his fragile ego. Avoid any conversation that doesn't allow him to be the hero of the story. Never listen to his story then try to "one-up" him with an adventure tale of your own. Allow the Aries man to feel like he's the most fascinating man you've ever conversed with.

A sure bet to keep him hooked is through pure flattery. The Ram doesn't mind if you sing his praises night and day. Just remember not to go overboard. Aries is the typical hunter, and you need to be his prey. If you start to look like you're trying too hard, he might bolt. As long as your flattery is low-key and he doesn't suspect it's a line, there's a good chance he'll ask you out before the night is through.

When it's time to plan that first date, let him take the lead. If you have some strong opinions about where you would like to go, be creative. Find a way to make the suggestion while still letting him feel like it was all his idea. You don't ever want to deflate this man's ego. The Aries ego is fragile; he's super-sensitive, especially about himself.

Because he often becomes infatuated, his sexual attractions are formed quickly. He gets off on the sensations of spur of the moment attractions.

If you get past the getting to-know-you stages and progress to sex with an Aries man, get ready for a wild ride.

Keeping Him Happy

- Make him the center of your universe.
- Be adventurous, spontaneous, funny and smart.
- Have your shit together. He needs a woman he can admire.
- Take him dancing. He loves to move his body in front of a large audience.
- Share his interests.
- Keep him on his toes because he bores easily.
- Never let your sex life get repetitive.
- Flatter him, but make sure it's sincere.
- Let him take control in the bedroom.
- Never nag or try to control him.

Sex

The Aries man's sexual appetite is voracious; so, ladies, pull out the Red Bull, because only the strong can survive an all-nighter. He's not going to hit it and roll over for a long snooze. Aries is a perfect gentleman, and will definitely make sure you get yours—a few times at least, or until you beg for mercy. It's important to him that when you report back to your "girlfriend club," his report will be nothing short of an A+.

When in bed with an Aries man, do not—I repeat, do not—try to take the lead. Aries needs to be in command. Always! It is best to follow his desires and appetites. Sometimes these desires might surprise you, but don't be afraid. To the Aries, sex and love are one. You might feel overwhelmed by his spirited approach to lovemaking, but try to relax and enjoy it. His energy is simply a reaction to the zealous intensity of his passion.

If you enjoy his kind of lovemaking, don't be afraid to show him your wild and unpredictable nature. Be ready for the ultimate sexual workout, and don't hold back in the bedroom if you want to keep your Aries man happy. He will make sure you experience new highs and lingering climaxes that extend beyond the boundaries of your imagination. Just be careful because if you fake being able to handle him the first time, he might not know it the second time, or the third time, and play a bit rough with you.

You must be willing to try new positions, since Aries likes to experiment and take things to the limit. He is writing his sex manual from scratch! He loves to initiate others into the pleasures of new and improved experiences. He will be ready to get busy in an elevator or a taxicab just as often as in the old traditional bedroom. He loves a challenge and will conquer you and your ideas.

On the flip side, the Aries man could benefit from discovering a more sensitive approach to the art of love. You must stroke his ego, let him lead the way, and at the same time, gently guide him into the more tender side of love and lovemaking.

Pampering him isn't a bad way to start. He would enjoy any evening designed specifically for him. Light some candles and show him your bed of rose petals. Rub some hot oil on his back and give him a sensual massage. If you get him excited, he'll take it from there.

Once you and your Aries man have found your sexual rhythm, don't slack up. With the Aries, there will always be women wanting to take your place. Don't ever think you've got him and you can relax with all this sex, stilettos, makeup, rock climbing and stuff. Get too comfortable, and your Aries will be off searching the next prize. You must be a woman with endless energy to handle this high-intensity lover.

Aries Turn-Ons

- Silk sheets
- Multiple orgasms
- Suck him until he cums—then swallow!
- Let him tie you up
- Play the damsel in distress
- Flatter him
- Loud acknowledgements during orgasms
- Red lingerie
- A leather whip for a present (and remember, he will use it!)
- The thrill of almost getting caught

Moving On Without Drama

First of all, the Aries ego will have a problem with you wanting to end the relationship, so just remember the number one rule: Let the Aries male drop you, never drop him . . . not if you want to live, bear children or fall in love again. The Ram won't be jealous like the Scorpio or hurt like the Capricorn; he will be in a blinding rage. Whatever you do, make him feel like the breakup was all his idea.

One friend of mine decided to take the Aries back to the hot club where they'd met months earlier. Once the Aries was surrounded by his adoring female fans, he quickly forgot all about her and moved on that very night. These males are usually on the lookout for the next big thing, so getting them to end things isn't usually that hard.

There are plenty of things you can do (or not do) to turn him off before you even bring him into the club. The best way to get rid of an Aries is to bore him, ignore him and refuse to whore for him. Leave the life of the party behind, and prefer to stay at home watching reality television. When he wants to talk about something that's important to him, turn up the volume on the TV and dismiss his feelings. That will be more than his ego can bear.

Aries wants his woman to look put-together all the time, so start wearing your baggy sweats and stop doing your hair. If he's still interested in sex even when you're looking your worst, use the tired old "I have a headache" line, or even worse, tell him you're not in the mood. At that point, you can be sure that his eye will be wandering the moment he steps foot in the club. You won't have to leave this man; he'll already be gone.

When you are done, be absolutely sure you are finished, because the Aries won't want anything to do with you ever again. When it comes to love, he dives into an affair positive that this is the only true love he'll ever know. But when it's done, dead and buried, he'll quickly start all over again with a new sister, and trust that this relationship will flow just as if it's his first time ever. As far as he's concerned, every time he falls in love is the first time. No matter how many romantic mistakes he makes, he is sure that Mrs. Right is out there somewhere. Just remember that with the Aries man, there is no Mrs. Second Chance.

Compatibility

ARIES

Aries Man/Aries Woman

If an Aries woman is in need of that late-night booty call and gets the phone number of a compliant Aries man, she should keep him on speed dial. This sexual encounter is bound to burn down the house. "Hit it and quit it" is best when two Aries get together. The sex is so good they won't want to leave the bed.

However, outside of the bedroom, the challenge is that both can be selfish people. Aries wants to be number one, so when two of them are involved, they will actually go to verbal blows over that alone. They get so involved in their goals that they forget to focus on their partner.

The Aries man is in touch with his boyish quality, and will work the charm factor, but the Aries female won't be impressed with the Peter

Pan thing. She also won't go for playing second fiddle to this man who likes to dominate.

Like her male counterpart, the Aries woman does not hide her desire to be powerful. She wears her sexiness like a coat of armor and dares anyone to mess with her, even her Aries man. The male Aries will love the idea of this hot, sexy-woman on the back of his Harley until she starts to give directions.

Both are straightforward, and they'll always be clear about where they stand, so as long as each is cool with the whole "friends with benefits" arrangement, this duo can produce fireworks. But the Aries is easily hurt, because beneath that tough, controlled exterior is a fragile ego. So, if one of these Aries is interested in a more committed relationship, he or she might get deeply hurt. Aries are "me" kind of people, so a long-term relationship between two of them is almost impossible.

Aries Man/Taurus Woman

Talk about different speeds. This relationship may not last long, but Ms. Taurus will enjoy her Aries man as he pushes her sexually to places she only dreamed of. These two can have a very exciting sexual encounter as long as he doesn't rush her. She desires slow, passionate foreplay, for which he doesn't have a lot of time.

Mr. Aries should learn to be patient with Ms. Taurus. There is no need to move from appetizer to dessert so quickly. And the payout will be great for his ego. Aries will enjoy watching Ms. Taurus reach an orgasmic state. She will climax and climax and climax.

These two are a perfect lovemaking match. Ms. Taurus is charmed by his enthusiasm for adventure, both in and out of the bed, and she's quick to tell him. This works well for the Aries man, who loves to have his ego stroked. However, because fire and earth are normally not an easy combination, it's probably best as a fling.

Aries Man/Gemini Woman

Oh, the joy of flirtation is no stranger to either of these zodiac signs. They each enjoy lovemaking and are up for the challenge of trying various new positions. This makes the Aries man and Gemini woman's sex tape one you would pay to watch. These two could have quite a successful relationship, since sex is something that they both love.

The Aries man loves control, and the Gemini woman will appreciate his directness between the sheets. The Gemini woman's ego is big enough that she doesn't have a problem allowing him to feel like he's in control. But he shouldn't take that love-struck look on her face as true. It might be just an act, because no matter what she wants him to think, the Gemini woman will always feel like she's the head diva in charge.

She can definitely make him believe she has fallen deeply in love, but the Aries man should remember that she comes with a twin, and things may change as soon as the other twin emerges. The Aries man should get to know both of them before he settles in for a long-term relationship.

Aries Man/Cancer Woman

Sexually, this duo can have strong passion and power—that is, initially. A Cancer woman has no problem trying out new sexual ideas with the Aries man.

When the relationship moves beyond sexual, the challenges begin. Ms. Cancer will quickly tire of Mr. Aries' ego and need for control. She's a homebody and a family-first kind of woman who likes things to be nice and easy. She will find the Aries man challenging and high maintenance, which is the opposite of what interests her in a man. His blunt personality will be especially hard for her to deal with.

Cancer is quite sensitive, so the Aries has to remember to choose his words carefully if he would like to keep her around. She will give him all the attention he desires, both in and out of the bedroom, and nurture his mind and body into passionate bliss. However, his roaming eye and flirtatious nature will have Ms. Cancer upset and ready to retreat back into her crab shell.

A Cancer woman broods in silence, eventually exploding, which is annoying to the Aries, who likes his woman to be easygoing. Eventually, these two won't be able to deal with how badly matched they are. They'll find themselves longing for something a little less dramatic, and the relationship will come to an end.

Aries Man/Leo Woman

"Look at me!"

"No, over here! Look at me!"

Both the Aries and the Leo demand all the attention in the room, which means one of them will have to find another room to hang out in. Leo is king (or queen) of the jungle, and Aries likes to think of himself as the first born, which will have them butting heads all day long.

These two fire signs are both very aggressive when it comes to sex. They have take-charge personalities, and the heat of their sexual passion can burn a hole in the mattress. You might find either of them hanging from the chandelier while trying out a great new sex position. If there is a possibility that they can reach a higher sexual peak, they'll try anything.

This dynamic duo's steamy sexual relationship will be a short-term one, though, unless Ms. Leo is willing to give in to the "Me!" wants of Mr. Aries. Or perhaps he can put his ego aside and step to the back while Ms. Leo shines. One of them must be willing to set ego aside if there is any hope for these two to light a fire and keep it burning for a while.

Aries Man/Virgo Woman

These two can't possibly be any more different, especially when it comes to their individual needs, so they should run from anything long-term. The Virgo likes things to be orderly and calm, while the Aries is a fly-by-the-seat-of-your pants kind of guy. Aries loves to go whenever, wherever with a moment's notice. Virgo doesn't go anywhere without checking it out first and making sure it's safe and she's dressed for the weather. And once she is dressed, she'll be left waiting for Aries, who is never on time—a big no-no in Virgo's book.

Sexually, Aries is adventurous and willing to try anything, while Virgo wants every sex act outlined and approved before she'll try it. She's not interested in swinging from ceilings. After all, how can she buy liability insurance for that act? Perhaps a quick, wham-bam-thank-you-ma'am in the bathroom stall of an American Airlines flight will give the Virgo woman that crazy jolt of excitement she's privately fantasized about but would never risk.

Aside from a quick fling, this mix is not recommended. Sexually, mentally, emotionally and physically, these two are polar opposites, and who needs life to be this hard?

Aries Man/Libra Woman

The Libra woman needs balance and harmony in order to feel happy, and the Aries likes his life to be off center. The Libra needs to be surrounded by beautiful things (which accounts for her shopaholic ways) while the Aries man is still rocking a pair of acid-washed denims that he believes fit him perfectly. She needs to have her life clothed in luxury down to the $4 bottle water, while the Aries doesn't see anything wrong with shopping for groceries at the 99-cent store.

Unlike the spontaneous Aries man, the Libra woman is meticulous and needs everything well-planned. She can be fussy and inflexible. So what if you broke your foot? You're not going to ruin her plans, so come along. Hop, hop!

The best thing they have going for them is that Ms. Libra enjoys all the freaky sex her Aries partner can dish out. Sure, it must be wrapped in a nice box called romance, but since they both want approval from their partner and they love being in love, Mr. Aries might not mind delivering it just the way she wants. If Ms. Libra can keep her Aries man in the bedroom and sexed up, she might not notice those orange pants he was wearing when he entered the house.

Aries Man/Scorpio Woman

Hot, hot, hot, and lots, lots, lots. What other reason would these two have to get together? They each like to experiment with positions, places and new things that are too embarrassing to even tell their best friends. Together they reach orgasms like you could only imagine. But that's the positive side of this coupling.

Since the Aries man needs to be the boss and the Scorpio woman is strong-willed and needs to be in control, there are always slamming doors and broken dishes in this relationship. Scorpio is intense, while Aries is easygoing, especially when things are going his way. Mr. Aries will have to put up a good fight to stay on top—and that does not mean only in the bed. Major problems happen when neither of them wants to give in.

If these two strong-willed people can make it to the bed or the couch or wherever, the sex might just be worth all the trouble. With this pairing, sex conquers all. If they stay naked and avoid any real power struggles, they've got the formula for a freaky, fun-filled three-week stand.

Aries Man/Sagittarius Woman

These two love movement and being on the go. If they could just slow down a bit and give their relationship the attention it deserves, they could stand a long-term chance. Their opposite personalities complement each other very well. Aries needs to be in complete control, and Sagittarius secretly wants a man to control her. So, when her Aries partner wants to be on top, she's happy to oblige. She will give her Aries man all the attention he desires, as well as all the sex.

Sex can be quite hot, since they never say no to anything in the bedroom. However, quickies seem to work best, since they always have someplace to go. These two are super social and will keep the party going long after the music stops.

Aries Man/Capricorn Woman

These two are very different. Capricorn wants a low maintenance man who allows her to be her workaholic self. Aries needs to be the biggest priority in his woman's life, and won't stand to come second to anything, including work. Already a recipe for disaster.

If these two even make it to the point of living together, things will only get worse. The Capricorn woman likes her home to be sacred, and won't stand for the Aries' constant parade of friends showing up unannounced. If Cap wants a stable man who has his finances in order, she's headed for just the opposite with this Aries partner.

Things aren't much better in the bedroom. A Capricorn woman can discuss the latest news topic for hours, and she'll dare to disagree with her Aries man. While this type of arguing might lead to some heated sex, it's not likely. The Aries man, who is always ready to hit it, will have to endure the Cap's way of doing things: discreet, familiar, and routine. There will be no bondage or chandelier swinging with these two, unless Aries proves he'll keep his big mouth shut and never tell for as long as he lives.

Yeah, if these two get together at all, this is a quick, horny night that should be left at that.

Aries Man/Aquarius Woman

The Aquarius woman is quite the cool one, but like the Aries man, she appreciates passion and great, freaky sex. These two will have no problem igniting each other's fire. With the interesting combination of sex and friendship, things are never dull with this pair.

Problems come when the Aquarius expects her partner to be a rebel and learns that the Aries is surprisingly traditional. He doesn't like to rock the boat at all.

The Aquarius female is a humanitarian and likes to give back to society, which the Aries won't mind, as long as it's not taking time away from him. Aries needs lots of attention from his woman, but the Aquarius needs lots of space and can't be bothered feeding compliments to that that hungry Aries ego all the time.

As long as they start each day with sex, they'll be less focused on all the things that don't work with this couple.

Aries Man/Pisces Woman

The take-charge Aries male works well sexually with the Pisces female. The two love sex, and the Fish will do anything in the world to make her man happy. Pisces might not plan for a kinky night. She much prefers for their sex to take place in a private location. But if it flows in that direction, she will gladly go along. She doesn't mind letting her Aries man take the lead, and his ego feeds off of this.

Outside of the bedroom is where these two run into problems. Pisces is always on the lookout for her Prince Charming, but the Aries man is not trying to be a part of the daydreamer fantasy. Pisces has a thin skin, and will be hurt by the constant absences of her cheating Aries. She craves a devoted partner who wants to be far away from the crowd, but the Aries man is only comfortable when he's center stage. Even the wild sex won't be enough to keep these two from breaking each other's hearts.

Famous Aries Men

MARCH 21–APRIL 19

Billie Dee Williams—April 6, 1937
Kenneth Babyface Edmonds—April 10, 1958
Eddie Murphy—April 3, 1961
Suge Knight—April 19, 1965
Flex Alexander—April 15, 1970
Martin Lawrence—April 16, 1965

Taurus

April 20–May 20

Your Taurus Man

Let's cut to the chase with the Taurus man, which is just the way he likes things done. Taurus is a no-nonsense guy who's not trying to waste his time with silly, flighty women. He is a dependable, strong brother who can take care of his business, easily stepping past the fluff to get to a real woman.

You'll notice that the single Taurus man is constantly being set up on dates, mostly by his exes. No one can understand why he's still single when he has so many of the qualities women search for in a man. The problem is that he is extremely picky.

That woman you ran into him with at that restaurant? Well, she's been dating him for six months, but you wouldn't know it by the formal way you were introduced. Yeah, she's still trying to maneuver her way into his heart. When this man introduces a female as "his woman," you can be sure she has passed the many prerequisite tests and patiently waited for him to claim her as his own.

Taurus wants to have that perfect relationship where the roles are clearly defined: he is the man and she is the woman. Not many Taurus men can do the stay-at-home dad thing. Taurus wants a woman who is exciting and sexy, but very feminine and well dressed. He wears the pants and expects his woman to not only wear the dress, but to accessorize it with killer heels and delicate jewelry.

When it comes to his ideal woman, he's expecting nothing short of perfection, and why not? After all, he's worked hard on himself to be a great earner and a BMW (black man working). He expects the same from his partner. But he's not looking for a submissive sister who has no goals and aspirations of her own. He'll spend a lifetime searching for his perfect counterpart, as soft as he is hard, as sexy as he is virile, and as classy as he is dignified.

Taurus will also want to know that his woman has her financial game tight before he considers a future with her. He is all about financial security and creature comforts. He lives to make a lot of money. People who don't know him may put him down as materialistic, but that would not cover the whole truth. The Bull needs to make money and surround himself with the trappings of wealth in order to feel safe and valuable in the world.

He came into this world recognizing his need to work hard and live well. Some people can fly by the seat of their pants and not worry about the big picture, but not the Bull. He is not a risk-taker. He'll never squander your fortune on a whim. And you can bet that all of his investments are stable, with long-term results. Taurus is not a man looking to make a quick buck. He does everything with an eye toward the future.

One major downfall of Taurus's practicality is that he can be very sensitive about his money. If you've ever been accused of being a gold digger, stay far away from Taurus. This is not a man who believes in handouts, and he might not be all that generous with gifts. But don't take it personally. It doesn't mean he doesn't care about you. It's just that he's trying to save for his children, and his children's children...

He works hard for his money and will expect other people to do the same. Taurus is a happy, go-with-the-flow brother until you start messing with his money, then he's a stressed out, rigid, angry individual. It doesn't matter how much he has or how little; this is not a brother who will appreciate you counting his money. So if you need to hit him up for a loan, you better come with a well-thought-out, sensible repayment plan, and if you're a day late making good on your loan, he'll write you off as a deadbeat who he can't trust. He's not someone who believes in the mixing of money and friendship or family.

Taurus's strict nature carries over into other aspects of his life too. Taurus is the sign of the bull, and if there is one trait all Taurus men have in common, it's stubbornness. It doesn't mean he can't bend a little to give you what you need, but if it's a choice between what you want and what he wants, then you are going to lose. He's not mean or obnoxious about it, he's just a man's man, and he doesn't have time to pretend that he's something he's not, including flexible. He can have a terrible temper when you push him out of his comfort zone, so it's best to learn how to avoid those moments.

One of the greatest qualities the Taurus man possesses is patience. While it might wear you out waiting for him to stake his claim to your heart, that same patience comes in handy in other areas. He will be patient with you and with his kids. This makes him good father/husband material, so if you think you can handle the more difficult aspects of his personality, then it's best to make your intentions known.

He isn't into a woman who plays hard to get, so if you're interested in Mr. Taurus, you better be up front and show it. If not, he may lose any desire for you and go on to the next woman. And trust that there is always a next woman waiting in the wings for him. Taurus is a chick magnet, and because he genuinely loves women, they flock to him. Any woman interested in this man has to realize he comes with a stack of friends who are all his exes and who would sleep with him again in a heartbeat.

But even when he finds a quality woman worth his time, he's not going to rush into a relationship with anyone. He's the man, and he takes his time deciding if you are the one. You may grow frustrated waiting for the Bull to treat you as something more than a friend with benefits. Taurus is the kind of man you may have to give up in order to have.

If he decides that you are the one for him, he will pursue you to the end of the earth. And once you two hook up, you can bet on your life being vastly improved. The Bull knows how to love a woman in a way that'll have you singing all the old school love songs and daydreaming about him. Taurus is incredibly romantic, and knows how to make a woman feel like the most desired creature in the world. In spite of all his stubborn traits and tight spending habits, this is a brother who has skills. If you can get him, then do yourself a huge favor and keep him.

Let's Get It Started

When you meet a Taurus, he'll be the one at a huge party, leaning against the bar, watching the crazy action around him with an amused look on his face. But just because he's amused doesn't mean he's impressed. It takes a lot to impress him, so be prepared to work for his attention.

Be warned that if you hang out with a Taurus man, it's best to keep it real. He's not the type to go for a woman who puts on airs and pretends she's all that. Taurus is looking for a regular girl who can chill with him at home on the sofa. He's low key and prefers life to be nice and easy. In other words, show him that you can keep it drama free, and you may get lucky.

He wants to be impressed with the woman he dates, so if you've won awards or finished first in law school let the Taurus know immediately. He's a material guy, so if you are interested in the finer things in life, let him know that without bragging. Show him pictures of your vacations, but if they include your ex-boyfriend don't bother to drag them out. He doesn't like to be in competition with other men, so don't put him in that position. And by all means, unless you are Def Comedy Jam funny, save the jokes for another time. Taurus is not looking for a silly woman.

If you do catch his eye and he asks you out, don't beat around the bush like you're so busy. If you're interested in dating a Taurus, just say yes, because he won't ask you again.

For your first date, expect him to take you to a nice restaurant with great food. This is the sign of a man who knows food and appreciates it. If he takes you to a fancy French restaurant and you spend the night bragging about how you ate at the chef's other place in Paris, he'll smile and nod pleasantly. He'll pay the check and have you home alone before dessert. Please save your bragging for a Leo male.

If you manage to make it to a second date, consider inviting him to your place. Remember that this is a man who is looking at you as a potential long-term partner, and he wants a woman who will mold to the traditional roles in the home. This means you should clear away all the clutter, sweep the dust from under the couch, and change the sheets on your bed just in case.

Before he arrives, be sure to put on your sexiest, most feminine outfit and get your hair and makeup just right.

If your man shows up with flowers, be sure to let him know how much it's appreciated. Any time he gives you a gift, remember it's his choice. Don't ask for something, especially something he's not willing to give. He'll feel put upon and start to freeze you out.

When it comes to what food to serve to your Taurus man, this is not the time to order in from Boston Market. Put on some smooth jazz and treat him to a tasty, home-cooked meal. Show him you have the skills to prepare a meal he would look forward to coming home to.

Now, what about dinner conversation? That's easy. One of the best ways to interest the Bull is to describe your assets and your financial portfolio. Being anything other than practical about money makes him extremely uncomfortable.

While you have him in your house, show him anything you collect that's valuable (and I don't mean the shot glasses from the fifty states). The Taurus man appreciates the finer things, and he likes to know that not only does his woman appreciate them, but she has the financial means to acquire them for herself. Show him that you've got yourself together, and you just might be able to take this thing to the next level.

Keeping Him Happy

- Never—and I mean never—nag him.
- Be drama free.
- Cook a fabulous dinner and let him see that you're a nester.
- Treat him like Prince Charming.
- Let him know you're stable.
- Give him lots of love.
- Compliment him on his fashion sense.
- Share similar family values.
- Be nice to his family.
- Always look exceptional.

Sex

The Taurus male started having sex way before any other boys in the neighborhood and he learned early how to please a woman. The trouble is that once he had his technique down and it worked, he didn't bother to add any new routines. He's almost ritualistic about it, doing the same things in the same order. The right woman can lead him into the darker realms of sex, especially threesomes, but his natural instinct is to play it safe. In general, this brother likes to stay on solid ground. So, if you're a woman into experimenting and changing things up, Taurus might not be the man for you.

The good news is that the tricks he does know involve giving plenty of pleasure to his woman. He is a slow and steady lover, who can start with the toes and work up to the top, taking lots of time to please each and every part of you. Don't bother to rush him; he's going to do it his way. To him, sex is like having Italian food in Italy: you take all day to enjoy your meal. If you're trying to get some fast food out of this brother, you're missing the best part.

If you've just come in from the gym, he won't want you to shower. The Taurus man is turned on by body funk, and likes a woman who smells fragrant. He wants to experience all of you—your smell, your touch, your taste. He finds your scent erotic, and it turns him on as he licks your inner thighs and tastes the salty sweat seeping from your pores. You might as well relax because he'll stop at your vagina and stay all day long, bringing you from one orgasm to another.

When it comes to intercourse, he can be incredibly romantic. He does love the idea of doing it outdoors, in the woods, or on the beach. But wherever you do it, this is the man who will flip you over, bend you into a pretzel, and turn you out. He enjoys building the sexual tension until you're both begging to be satisfied, and that's when you'll really see that the bull is the most sensual sign of the zodiac.

Taurus is a man who won't finish until he puts you to sleep. This man lives to please a woman in bed. But don't let yourself get "addick-ted" because you might not be the only one enjoying his skills. Taurus believes he can please every woman, and he often sets out to prove it by entertaining lots of lovers while he's on his quest to find the perfect wife material. All I have to say is don't do it if you can't imagine walking away, because with the Taurus, sex may be all he's offering.

Taurus Turn-Ons

- Watch him masturbate.
- Plenty of foreplay.
- Wear skimpy, sexy undergarments.
- Ask him to describe how he wants you to please him.
- Let him take the lead.
- Go down on him for a long time.
- Slow and steady sex.
- Nibble his ears.
- Lick his neck.
- Full body massage with oils.

Moving On Without Drama

The easiest and least painful way to extract yourself from a Taurus is to become bored with him sexually. His ego won't be able to take it. This man needs to be loved body and soul, and if you make it clear you're not available for that, he may let you go easily. The most important thing to remember is that a Taurus man is not easily shaken, so you have to be brutally obvious. Flirt with other men, become real cheap with your affection, and back away slowly. We're talking about leaving one of the most possessive signs of the zodiac.

Of course, if you've been together a while, your Taurus man may do everything he can to keep the relationship together. Be prepared for this because he can be incredibly charming. If you're not on your game, he will convince you that there are no other great men left out there, and certainly no one who will love you as much as he does.

If you're still determined to leave him, there's one surefire way to get him to happily show you the door: become a big spender—with his money. When he gives you money to pay the household bills, spend a large chunk of it on frivolous things for yourself. Go ahead, get your hair and nails done on his dime. When he tries to talk to you about it, tell him you're tired of being told how to spend your money. Take the reins and announce that you want to start making some of the decisions in this relationship, including the financial ones. This will drive the Taurus man crazy and he'll remind you that it was his money, not yours. Simply roll your eyes and tell him that once the money touches your hands, it becomes yours.

You won't have to do much more. Taurus is a man who doesn't like to part with his cash. If you make him believe this is the new you, it won't be long before he's moving on to greener pastures.

Compatibility

TAURUS

Taurus Man/Aries Woman

These two both like sex, but their styles are too different to make a lasting connection.

Taurus man looks at each sexual partner as a potential life partner. He's romantic and sensual, and the better the sex, the more he wants it to lead to a relationship. His lovemaking is masculine, passionate, and erotic, and he can go on for hours. When the lovemaking is over, he wants a woman who'll stay at home with him and keep the bed warm.

Aries woman, on the other hand, can have sex just for the sake of sex. Not every partner is someone she wants to spend time with after the act is done. She'll hang out long enough to get in a quickie, but then it's on to the next party. She likes to be on the go, with a steady stream of admirers.

Taurus wants a sexy, feminine woman who can conform to his idea of perfection. But Aries needs her freedom and can't be tied down, domesticating. Taurus is a good long-term or marrying type of man, and if he's smart, he will stay clear of the ever-fleeting Aries Woman.

Taurus Man/Taurus Woman

Imagine watching and waiting for a large pot of water, with an extremely low flame come to a boil. In the meantime, you can watch a football game, play a hand of cards, surf the Internet and Christmas shop for a family of twenty. Well, you can do all that and more before two Tauruses get hot and heavy under the sheets. They know what it takes to satisfy each other, but they are slow and cautious.

The Taurus female is a material girl, but the Taurus male prefers to keep his money close to him and not waste it on bling and shoes. She's outgoing and fun and can shine at any social gathering, but he wants to be the one with the dominant personality. These two are notoriously stubborn, which means something has to give, but unfortunately, it won't be either of these Tauruses. This is one of those "been there, am that" kind of attractions, so I suggest these Bulls pull up a mirror and love the one they're with—themselves—and let the other one go.

Taurus Man/Gemini Woman

Sex can go either way with these two, so when they find a rhythm that works, you'll find them beneath the sheets. They prefer to be butt naked, without any lingerie, so they can oil up their bodies and rub them against each other. Kissing, rubbing, licking, the touch of skin turns on this pair to the point where they won't need to go much further.

Once they've started, Gemini women are uninhibited and move quickly, but the Taurus man is slow to the race and needs to perk up lest he gets left behind. The Gemini can quickly become bored while waiting for Taurus to express his emotions. The Twins want praise and compliments and a road dog to hang with them, while Taurus prefers a partner to domesticate with at home. Gemini loves the sound of her own voice so much that the earthy Taurus grows bored with her bragging ways. It's mostly frivolous stuff that can frustrate the Taurus man. If longevity is what you're seeking, this is the wrong ride, because this match is headed in the direction of a one-night stand.

Taurus Man/Cancer Woman

The nature of these two is to take things slow. Their rhythms are mellow, and they can be lazy together. The Taurus man is a cuddling kind of brother, which works well with the Cancer woman, who is a nurturer. When it comes to sex, the action will happen in a safe, familiar place, like home. If the Taurus man gets adventurous, he may want to try some new positions with his sensitive Cancer woman. She will go along, but he should never expect her to be the one to initiate.

Sex is not just a physical thing for them; both crave a deeper connection that makes sex a more fulfilling experience. The Taurus man has the ability to handle the moody Cancer woman, and because he's solid, he'll always give her a safe place to land. Long hours of lovemaking can be expected from him, which is a sure way to level out her roller-coaster emotions by helping her to work off some of her fear.

This duo could actually find themselves together for a lot longer than a one-night stand because each instinctively knows what the other needs in order to be happy.

Taurus Man/Leo Woman

Strong animals, the Bull and the Lion, mean strong sex. Together this duo will share lots of good times, both in and out of the bed. They have similar tastes when it comes to sex, and each needs a lot in order to feel powerful.

Since the Taurus man is confident and can handle a forceful kind of loving, he's right up this Leo woman's alley. She likes her men to be all men, with nothing fluffy about them. When a Leo meets her sexual match, she'll do anything he wants—if only to prove that no other female comes close to her performance level. She's highly competitive in the bedroom, and will go past her comfort zone, trying S&M and even a threesome if she's challenged.

Unfortunately, outside of the bedroom, the Leo female won't do anything she doesn't want to do. This sister isn't going to stay home and cook dinner every night; she wants to march her new Prada platforms down to the disco and get her groove on. Leo can leave the Taurus feeling neglected with her "front and center" personality.

Both Taurus and Leo like to be in control, so it's a constant battle of wills, with neither giving in. Let them keep this in the bedroom because once their clothes are back on, they include the boxing gloves.

Taurus Man/Virgo Woman

These two can be a calming and dependable (in other words, boring) duo. The fact that Virgos need to take their time is comforting for Taurus, who is also likes to approach things from a slower pace. Neither wants to risk being wrong about a relationship, which helps them build up a trust. They want guarantees before they open up and give their hearts.

This duo will not experience a lot of passion in the bedroom, at least initially. Taurus is more sexually adventurous. Virgo can be a little sex-by-the-books, but once Taurus gets her in the mood, lovemaking can be gratifying. We're not talking feet on the ceiling, multi-orgasmic kind of pairings. It's more "slow and steady wins the race" sex. They're the couple that sticks with the missionary position, perhaps doggie style on Tuesday, but that works for them.

With a desire to fulfill each other's needs sexually and emotionally, these two could either be best friends or married forever. These earth signs are good together and they know that fireworks and passion are fleeting, but real, solid love can last forever. Their relationship will grow and get better as time passes.

Taurus Man/Libra Woman

These two are no strangers to romance, and they love late-night dancing and candlelit dinners. Taurus prefers a woman who is ultra feminine and lets him be the man, so Libra's elegance and beauty is a perfect match. She will enjoy being taken to fine restaurants and treated like a queen. Libra's sense of style is so great that her Taurus man will even agree to let her give him a much-needed makeover—and he'll only mind if it costs him lots of money.

They each like to keep it private when it comes to sex. Exhibition is for another duo; discretion is advised here. But the Libra should watch out. Taurus man loves a few moans, groans and perhaps a few loud yells to let him know he's hitting all the right spots. The Libra will have to tone down her need to have everything so perfect and elegant, and let the earthy Taurus man rock her world. He'll spend hours performing cunnilingus and making sure she's satisfied. That's reason enough to try to make this relationship work.

Unfortunately, this is a union that is often destined to fail, perhaps because they are not a challenge to one another.

Taurus Man/Scorpio Woman

Sex, sex, and more sex. What other reason is needed for these two to get together? Absolutely none. Sex is its own motivating factor.

The sexual tension these two share can be felt from across the room. The Scorpio woman is game for all kinds of tricks and kinky positions. She'll help the Taurus man get out of his box and try those wilder than normal positions he's been thinking about. On the flip side, he's a calming force for the intense, emotional Scorpio. Once she feels safe and loved, she'll do anything to make her partner happy. Together, they turn each other out.

Outside of the bedroom, these two are just as compatible. Give a Taurus man a whiff of a Scorpio woman, and he's sure to drop his guard. She's an achiever. If she wants something, she gets it—sex, money and knowledge. This is almost more than any Taurus man can resist.

This duo can be a force to be reckoned with, in a long- or short-term relationship.

Taurus Man/Sagittarius Woman

The Sagittarius woman is eager to please. Sexually, that is. She's game to try many different and new positions, although the Taurus man might want to discuss sex toys before he whips them out. The Sag woman will probably want to go a few rounds at least, so the strong, masculine sexuality of the Taurus male is a good fit for her. She'll also appreciate his need to lavish her with plenty of attention, as long as it's sincere.

Unfortunately, Taurus will want more from Sagittarius than she is willing to give. After all, she is freedom-loving and likes to keep things light. The Taurus man should never try to put a tracking device on this sister. If he gives her some air, things should work, at least for a while. As long as she's happy, there's not much chance the Sagittarius woman will cheat. The Taurus man should enjoy this one while it lasts, though, because even if he is holding it down in the bedroom, their needs are too different for this pair to make it past the short term.

Taurus Man/Capricorn Woman

Both these earth signs need a partner who is real and not on some fake, fronting thing. They sense this about each other, and will feel a kinship that leads to great trust between them. This combination has a chance at a relationship full of good fun, stimulating conversation, and a life free of debt and drama.

Once they get comfortable, the sex can be wonderful, but he'll have to be patient. She loves sex, but tends to stick within her comfort zone. The Taurus man will have to put some thought into it if he wants to get the Capricorn lady to a place where she can throw caution to the wind. If he does that, he will enjoy the benefits of a sexual partner who keeps coming back for more. Sex with this duo is not usually accompanied with fireworks, but if both have been around a while, it could be a little freakier than normal.

A Capricorn woman can feel safe with a Taurus man. This is a relationship that has marriage potential.

Taurus Man/Aquarius Woman

Get out the boxing gloves. These two will duel until the end, and may the best zodiac sign win. Both signs are strong-willed and quite different. Aquarius wants to change the world, but Taurus is comfortable with the status quo and won't appreciate being asked to look at the world differently.

If they can get past debating about who is to do what, a Taurus man and an Aquarius woman can actually enjoy a night between the sheets. Taurus can sometimes be sexually uptight, but the Aquarius is the sexual freak of the zodiac. She's not afraid to make the first move, and she has no problem jumping on top and riding her man. The Taurus man might be a little put off by her aggressive nature and her spontaneity. If an Aquarius woman can find a way to get the Taurus to lighten up, they will have a night of passion. Unfortunately for this couple, it won't be enough, and chances are they'll never make it past that first night.

Taurus Man/Pisces Woman

These two are a sexually soothing couple who have no problems meeting each other's needs. They are both homebodies, which is great, because that's where the bed happens to be. But every part of the Pisces woman's body exudes sexuality, so she might just surprise her Taurus man and convince him to do it in that beanbag chair in his friend's guest house.

Taurus will have to pay attention to Pisces's lack of concern for money, though, since she thinks it grows on trees. It will be Taurus's job to take care of the finances so they don't wind up kicked out of the poor house.

This might be the only pitfall of a relationship between a Taurus man and a Pisces woman. If he can keep her spending under control, this can be a dynamic duo, hot and sexy and in it for the long haul.

Famous Taurus Men

APRIL 20–MAY 20

Akon—April 30, 1973
Damon Dash—May 3, 1971
Djimon Hounsou—April 24, 1964
Hill Harper—May 17, 1966
Cedric The Entertainer—April 24, 1964
Darryl M. Bell—May 10, 1963
Darius McCrary—May 1, 1976
Emmett Smith—May 15, 1969
Kenan Thompson—May 10, 1978
Ving Rhames—May 12, 1959
Derek Luke—April 24, 1974
GianCarlo Esposito—April 26, 1958
Master P—April 29, 1967
Chris Brown—May 5, 1989

Gemini

May 21–June 21

Your Gemini Man

The Gemini is one of the hardest signs to figure out. One minute he is a calm man-child, willing to let you have your way, and the next, he is a worldly, powerful man who wants to be in charge. He is often accused of being two separate people, but it's not his fault. After all, his symbol is the Twin, two individuals fighting for control. The truth is, your Gemini man is at least four people, and that's on a calm day. He emotes like the wind, changing moods in the blink of an eye. But, please, whatever you do, don't call him a schizophrenic. He can't help being many different people, and when I say many, I mean twenty-four hours in a day can offer up twenty-four different personalities. If you watch closely, you'll notice that he even changes during his sleep.

This man is ruled by the planet Mercury. At turns, he is moody, intense, and fiery. In the next breath, he's also fun, outgoing and charming. All of these personalities don't stop him from being extremely popular and a must-invite party guest. He has that ability to make everyone in the room feel special. Nobody ever accused this man of being boring.

The Gemini man is easily one of the most fascinating, smooth men you'll ever come across and he knows it. He is a showman and loves any opportunity to entertain the masses, which is probably why many Geminis go into acting, music, or politics. When you see that brother holding a crowd's attention, informing them about the latest political crisis or drinking water disaster, you can bet he's a Gemini. The Gemini believes it is his duty to educate the masses about all past and current events. Before long, you'll wonder if the Gemini gets information for himself or to prove his intellect to others. It's probably a little bit of both. Secretly, he's deeply insecure and uses his loud voice and outgoing attitude to distract people from his own internal doubts about his self-worth.

The Gemini is a conversation whore and likes to take over any discussion. He can go for hours on intellectual stimulation, but you'll be aware that he'll rarely stay on one topic for long. In fact, one of his more noticeable character traits is a short attention span. He skims most issues, gathering enough information to be informed but not to be an expert. If you're really interested, you better be able to play a game of verbal hockey, moving from one topic to the next without long pauses. This man is like a comet, moving swiftly from one topic to another, one person to another, and one activity to another. He is an ever moving target, which makes it hard for things to stick to him.

This flighty nature means the Gemini man has a bad habit of putting too many eggs in too many baskets. He's always finding things that appeal to him, which leads to him taking on too many projects at once and not being able to see any of them through to the end. He'll give one thousand percent when he takes on a project, but that initial enthusiasm and commitment won't last. He'll become distracted by some other idea that is twice as fascinating and challenging as the last one. This may be why he changes jobs so often.

Speaking of employment, the Gemini man is great at earning a living through whatever he chooses to do. The problem is that when it comes to money, the Gemini doesn't take its value seriously. He believes he can always make more whenever he needs. It's like he uses money to test himself. He'll make it and waste it, as if he's trying to wind up in the poor house. It's not that he's interested in struggling or that he can live without money. He's just attracted to the challenge of having to start from broke again. Geminis are famous for going from rich to poor to rich again.

You might wonder where all his money goes. Well, Gemini is current and always obsessed with having the latest bling. If a new Mercedes with extra speed shows up on the market, he either has it already or he's figuring out how to get it. He's always on the hunt for the hottest restaurant, coffee house, ride, or clothing, and when a hot designer shows up on the scene, Gemini is first to rock the look. Gemini can be high maintenance and expensive.

But in spite of all of this, women of all ages are taken with the Twin because he has the answer to everything and comes across as Prince Charming. In his looks and his behavior, he exudes a confidence that just draws women to him. He's one of the most entertaining men on the planet and has an amazing sense of humor. Just try not to take the harem surrounding him too seriously. He can't help that women love him and he loves them back.

For the woman who does catch herself a Gemini man, she has her work cut out for her. Gemini demands lots of space and freedom. He's not the type of brother to call and check in to make a woman feel secure, and he's not known to show up on time. But paradoxically, he expects his woman to be at his beck and call, and to answer every time he blows up her PDA.

If you're looking for a homebody to cuddle up on the couch with you, then Gemini is definitely not the one. But if you're interested in an on-the-go man who will bring you from one social function to the next, who's always up for a party, then go for it. A Gemini man can be great in a crisis. He'll put out a fire, offer you shelter, and loan you money without ever complaining. Just make sure you're up for the challenge that is the Gemini man.

Let's Get It Started

Intellectual stimulation is the best way to get a Gemini to notice you (although a low-cut top and plenty of cleavage will help!) When you see him at a party surrounded by adoring women, make yourself stand out from the crowd and get his undivided attention. Come up with some great ideas about the war, the stock market, or the latest television hit in order to seduce him. Ask his opinion about something controversial.

The Gemini is turned on by your ability to argue with him, so start by challenging his stand on a topic. Brush up on this whole global warming thing, because he's sure to have an opinion about it. Don't be afraid to disagree with his political or religious beliefs.

Now, I'll give you warning. If you call this brother on the carpet about something, you better have your facts straight. To win an argument, you have to cite cases where your point has been proven. He's a smart man, and it takes an even smarter person to change his views. If you try to get into the emotional side of an argument, ignoring all the facts, he'll dismiss you as an idiot.

If you do catch his eye, work your magic quickly because you're not going to get a lot of time to show him what you're working with. This brother has a very short attention span, and will be off on some other tangent in no time. Your best bet is to engage all of his senses at once. Argue with his beliefs while you're refilling his wine glass and rubbing his shoulder with a soft, feminine touch. And be sure to stand in such a way that he has an unobstructed view of your best assets, which, hopefully, you keep in great shape with regular visits to the gym. Gemini men expect their women to be sexy even while being competitive.

If Gemini invites you on a date, let him make the plans, and know that it won't be dinner and a movie. Geminis are spontaneous, so don't be surprised if he offers to take you on a balloon ride. When it's your time to make the plans, you have to be spontaneous also in order to keep him interested. Invite him to something fun and outgoing, such as a murder mystery play. Find activities which engage his mind. Use your imagination to keep his attention and he'll reward you by making sure you have a great time.

Keeping Him Happy

- Take him to a book signing or anything intellectually stimulating.
- Rent a good documentary.
- Take a massage class and surprise him with a full-body massage.
- Find an adventurous hobby you can do together.
- Be creative, and never let things get too rigid or dull.
- Ask his opinion about something controversial.
- Bet on his favorite sports team.
- Plan a surprise vacation.
- Give him lots of space.

Sex

Sex with the Gemini man will be less about passion and more about the total experience. He's not so much into your experience as he will be interested in what you think of his experience with you. Think of him as a political candidate working to keep up his approval ratings.

When it comes to sex, the Gemini doesn't ever want to be hurried. He does appreciate a quickie, but it's more about having sex exactly the way he wants it. The problem is that he changes desires as often as he changes personalities. Remember, this sign is two people in one body, which means many different things can interest him at once. He likes sex to be spontaneous and varied. You have to be open-minded for the twins.

One of his favorites is the threesome because there are enough people to focus on both twins. He likes to have sex with one partner while he can watch another masturbate. He's also into S&M and toys; some you didn't even know were legal. If you think candlelight and oils next to the bed will turn him on, well, maybe you're not ready for the Gemini. The Gemini craves the excitement of taking everything to the next level.

If the Gemini brother invites you to his place, you can bet that there will be mirrors all around. He likes to watch the action while he's doing it. He enjoys porno because he likes to copy the moves of the actors on screen. Gemini might even try to outdo the professionals, so don't be surprised if he suddenly flips you into a pretzel to get a better angle.

He's not big on fellatio or cunnilingus because he likes to get down to business. If you think that guarantees you won't get off with the Gemini, then you're mistaken. He may start slowly, but before the sex is over, he'll have you writhing in excitement. During the act, Gemini will be taking notes to see if there is any way to increase the pleasure you two are having.

The problem with Gemini is that he can cool down as quickly as he gets hot. If this brother is giving you vibes that he's interested, I wouldn't play any games or try to make him chase you, because he won't. If you're looking for a deep, soulful sexual experience that bonds you as one, this is not the male. But if you want a brother who's down to try anything at least once, then hurry up and get yourself a Gemini before he moves on to the next woman.

Gemini Turn-Ons

- A tight body with a bubble butt
- The ability to hang with him
- Porno
- Sex with the lights on
- Group sex
- Gadgets
- Sex in weird places
- Sucking on his fingers and toes
- Doing it in the shower
- Variety

Moving On Without Drama

Breaking up with a Gemini isn't that hard, since he tends to lose interest in things quickly anyway. During meaningful conversations, give uneducated answers to his questions. Refuse to debate his opinions; instead, just tell him he's wrong and then shut down. If you do talk, hog the conversation and talk only about yourself, your opinions and your needs.

He'll also lose interest quickly if you fail to stimulate his other senses. Dress like a slob all the time and don't bother going to the gym. Take him to a corny, out of the way restaurant, where the service is bad and the food is worse. While you're there, order his food for him, then talk about how hot you think the waiter is. The Gemini ego will not allow him to be with a woman who isn't entirely focused on him. He needs to be the center of your universe.

What he doesn't want to be, though, is your whole world. He won't be able to stand it when you act insecure and check up on him all the time, expecting him to be accountable for his whereabouts. Act like a jealous lover. This will make him crazy—until you distract him with doubts about your own fidelity. Come home late with no explanation. Let him catch you texting someone, then act guilty. Hold whispered conversations on your cell phone, and this poor Twin will be beside himself in no time. Before you know it, your Gemini man has moved on to some new Harvard grad who stimulates his mind.

Once you decide you are done with the Gemini and give him his walking papers, don't waste any time trying to look back. Geminis are not known for second chances, especially when there are so many lovely ladies they wanted to holla at, and now they have the chance. Women love him and he knows it, so don't expect him to care too much that you're gone.

Compatibility

GEMINI

Gemini Man/Aries Woman

These two are in synch. They are sexually compatible, and are not likely to become bored in bed. Conversations about what turns them on can be expected, leading them to try out some of the things they've been talking about. They enjoy a variety of sexual pleasures, starting with oral sex. These two will joke and laugh in the bed, which can lead to even more sex.

Gemini wants to have sex to see how a woman reacts to him. The Aries wants to have sex to see if a man can turn her on. She knows that the Gemini may not satisfy her completely, but she's ecstatic that he hits all the right buttons. There might be some minor power struggles because the Aries woman needs to be in control, and secretly, so does the Gemini man. But if the sex is good and the Aries woman can provide her Gemini man with lots of space and freedom, there could be a long-term alliance between these two.

A celebrity couple that probably would have made this Aries/Gemini combination work for the long haul was Kidada Jones, Quincy Jones's daughter, and Tupac Shakur. Kidada was a famous "It girl," whose constant globetrotting kept the short-attention-spanned Gemini interested.

Gemini Man/Taurus Woman

Perhaps a short affair might be the answer for these two. Sex can be truly amazing or unquestionably bad, especially since these two have little if anything in common. Taurus is a homebody, and the Gemini always wants to be in a home, but not his own. Gemini likes to talk about everything, while Taurus prefers to talk only when things matter to her. Gemini can change like the wind, and Taurus needs consistency. Sexually, Taurus is a bit ordinary and slow for Gemini.

But don't get it twisted. When Gemini has finished talking and Ms. Taurus speeds up, they can get down with some wild and crazy sex. Gemini will insist on both toys and porno in order to keep him stimulated. Taurus lets her guard down for the Gemini, and will even try anal sex if he insists it turns him on.

But don't get caught up, Taurus. This will most likely not go beyond a one-night stand. Well, perhaps two nights.

Gemini Man/Gemini Woman

These two will definitely keep each other amused, if nothing else. Geminis like to talk, and with two of them, they spend so much time talking that they can forget to do anything else. When they do get around to sex, though, it's definitely not ordinary.

When this twosome gets together, (or should I say this foursome?) the vibrations in the room are high. Although they tend to bore easily in other areas, there are flames in the bedroom. Two Geminis will do anything sexually, if only to say they've had the experience. Gemini is the sign that likes to swing, so together, they will go to a party and turn out other people. Gemini likes the power of being sexually adventurous.

But as quick as those flames flare, so can their tempers. What was simple and sweet goes sour and chaotic quickly. The attraction to each other will fade, and they will eventually turn against each other. This intense coupling can burn out pretty quickly. Don't expect anything long-term.

Gemini Man/Cancer Woman

This duo can be a challenge. Cancer is a sensitive, sexually reserved person, while Gemini likes to be in love and loves outside stimulation. Gemini will have to get Cancer to release her sexual inhibitions, but when that happens, their physical attraction has the ability to lead to quite the sexual relationship.

Still, no matter how good the sex, this union is dangerous. Gemini will play a love game, and Cancer will take it seriously. Cancer needs approval, and she wants to believe this man is the prince she's been waiting for while she had to kiss all those frogs. Gemini can't be bothered with any fantasy world. Cancer can be clingy, wanting the Gemini to stay close, while the Gemini needs to have lots of space in order to feel comfortable.

A difference in temperaments will be a source of constant problems in bed. Cancer leans towards the sentimental side, while Gemini lays it on cool. They have a lot to learn from each other, but unless Gemini practices sensitivity and Cancer toughens up, a relationship between the two may not be the best idea.

Gemini Man/Leo Woman

The Leo woman can find the Gemini man very sexy. He will be entertaining and educating as he tells her stories about how the rest of the world is doing. Ms. Leo just needs to make sure she gives her man the freedom he needs. This shouldn't be a problem, though, since Leo needs to be surrounded by her own steady stream of male admirers. If Gemini doesn't have time to give her that kind of attention, then Leo may have to get a little something on the side to make up for the coldness of Gemini.

Although these signs can be a bit self-involved, neither one minds when the other one shines. They will take turns servicing and intriguing one another between the sheets. They are a passionate, kind couple who stimulate each other. Basically, they are a hot and fun duo, so a long-term sexual partnership is possible.

Gemini Man/Virgo Woman

Well, this one doesn't appear to be very promising. If you're looking for juicy, wild sex, put your glasses back on and continue reading. Together, these two are thinkers who are interested in the world around them, but for entirely different reasons. These two have busy minds, and because of all that thinking, might miss the boat when it comes to gritty-dirty sex.

Virgo wants to help make the world a better place, while Gemini simply wants to make his world better for him and those he loves. Gemini needs to focus more, and the Virgo needs to envision the larger picture. Virgo's pet peeve is lateness, and the Gemini is horribly bad at time management. Gemini would prefer it if Virgo let him run the show, but even a calm water sign wants to be in control. In other words, these two are quite opposite. The sex might be good, if these two could ever get past their differences and make it to the bedroom.

Gemini Man/Libra Woman

This relationship is suitable for a good friendship, which can turn into a buddy kind of sex. Gemini likes to keep it moving and Libra is the same way, which means neither gets tied down with neediness. This is a meeting of passion and intellect.

Libra is a romantic who wants someone permanent, but she might enjoy a jolt of wildness from her Gemini mate. Sex games and role playing are not a problem for Ms. Libra. Fishnet, black panty hose, and a pair of stiletto heels are no stranger to her. This will be fun for Gemini, but he should remember to romance her first, because she requires that.

Gemini is rarely on time and never calls to say he's late, which will drive Ms. Libra insane. Gemini never stops talking, which gets in the way of the famous Libra peace. He's a wild assortment of things and she's a classy, elegant kind of woman. Yet with all these differences, these two can enjoy each other's company. Think Payday candy bar, or sweet and sour sauce: an interesting combination.

Gemini Man/Scorpio Woman

Scorpio is focused; Gemini is, well, a bit fickle, distracted, and curious. Scorpio wants to know the real Gemini, which might be a li'l intimidating for him. The problem is that Scorpio needs to stay intrigued in the relationship. Once she's sorted through the conversation and played along with the sex games, if Gemini doesn't find a way to hold her interest, sex might lose its excitement.

In the bedroom, Scorpio likes to try everything from anal sex to group sex. This will be a huge turn-on for the Gemini. Ms. Scorpio will call Gemini on his sexual jibber-jabber. Once Gemini stops talking, that's when the fun begins. Scorpio is up for sexual games, and Gemini is able to bring it anytime, anyplace.

One major issue with the Gemini/Scorpio combination is the Twin's inability to be faithful. The possessive Scorpio can't deal with a man who cheats, and will turn from a rageful mate to an ice princess. There is no guarantee that Gemini Lenny Kravitz and Scorpio Lisa Bonet divorced because of the Gemini's Casanova tendencies, but what is obvious is that the deeply private Scorpio woman won't be interested in the Gemini man's need for constant female attention. In the end, these two are better off as friends.

Gemini Man/Sagittarius Woman

A Sagittarius female is outgoing, but she is also very private. A Gemini is very sociable, and he wants to be inside of her head, even when she has a need to have solitude. But even with this difference in temperament, these two can be quite compatible. Both are outgoing and love a challenge, which is why they can ignore their many differences.

When it comes to his need for movement and her need to be free, they work well together. It's easier for them to understand where their mate is and what they need. They like to travel together, even though Sagittarius eventually will want to settle down to a more stable relationship.

Sexually, they compliment each other and can be stimulating and intellectual. In many ways, they are understanding of each other and may spend time just chatting in the bed. This can sometimes last longer than the act of sex itself. Sagittarius is frustrated and interested in the Gemini man at the same time. Who is this creature, she might ask herself. Oral sex is the ticket to keep these two happy for a little while. Both will be blinded to their differences by the sexual heat.

Gemini Man/Capricorn Woman

Sorry, this is an unlikely pair. Ms. Capricorn is all reality and won't be interested in the Gemini's need for a flashy ride or diamond studs in his ears. Capricorn is a solid woman who wants to know that her man has a 401K and he's saving for the kids' college funds.

She won't be impressed with the Gemini intellect because few people are as research- driven as the Capricorn, and she'll know way more than the Gemini does on any subject. And if she doesn't, she'll get back to him with more information, which will piss him off. Gemini needs to be the smart one in a relationship, and with the Lady Cap, it's just not possible.

There can be chemistry between them, but sex might be a bit rigid and buddy-like. Perhaps the Gemini man can loosen up the Capricorn woman and get her to yell and scream. Gemini should try spanking her a few times to make her behave. He will have to work hard to make her laugh, but if he gets her to let go, it might lead to an entertaining roll in the hay.

Long-term, she's looking for a low-key, responsible man with high morals, who would never stray, and, well, that's not the Gemini.

Gemini Man/Aquarius Woman

Psychic ability seems heightened with this duo. Both love exploring sex, and will feel they know the other's sexual desires without them saying a word. Their sexual energies are compatible, so any fantasies kept hidden with previous partners, they can unleash them now. They can spend an entire afternoon exploring a few adult shops together. These two are so in tune mentally, they're sure to find new sexual toys to enhance every experience in bed.

The Gemini man and Aquarius woman give each other space, since both become claustrophobic when too much is demanded of them. Gemini loves how the Aquarius can be a part of a crowd and still preserve her individuality. Together, these two spend hours and hours engaged in conversation about all the mysteries of the universe.

One of the only issues will be that Aquarius is a humanitarian and the Gemini believes that charity begins and ends with him. He's not the type to want to give unless there is a photo op or some compliments and praise. She, on the other hand, doesn't want to be recognized for something she believes is her duty. But, if I had to bet some money, I'd risk it on this couple. This duo has a good chance of making it.

Gemini Man/Pisces Woman

Hot? No. More like lukewarm. With different rhythms, it won't be easy for these two to get lost in lust. They just don't have enough in common.

Her sensitivity and his fickleness just don't go together. Pisces needs a man who is always around and puts her first, but the Gemini has two others who take that number one spot—his twin personalities. Gemini wants to keep it easy, but the Pisces can be intense, especially when she's not placed high up on a pedestal.

Sex will work; not hot and steamy, but sex nonetheless. Gemini will need to learn to slow down between the sheets. Pisces's approach is a bit more relaxed, and she won't appreciate all that chatter.

Pisces wants Prince Charming, and Gemini wants to be major of the world. Yeah, let's avoid the fantasy that this can work.

Famous Gemini Men

MAY 21–JUNE 21

Notorious BIG—May 21, 1972
Thomas Mikal Ford—June 15, 1962
Mark Curry—June 1, 1960
Keith David—June 4, 1956
Faison Love—June 14, 1968
Deondre Whitfield—May 27, 1969
Ice Cube—June 15, 1969
Keenan Wayans—June 8, 1958
Brian McKnight—June 5, 1969
Tupac Shakur—June 16, 1971
Lenny Kravitz—May 26, 1964
Kanye West—June 8, 1977
Andre Benjamin—May 27, 1975
Prince—June 7, 1958
Carl Anthony Payne II—May 24, 1969

Cancer

June 22–July 22

Your Cancer Man

Cancer is referred to as the mother of the zodiac, whether male or female. When a man has so many feminine qualities, it may make you believe he is soft and not masculine, but that couldn't be further from the truth. The Cancer male should be appreciated for what he is—a natural parent who is nurturing in all his relationships.

Women flock to him because he is patient, attentive and deeply understanding. He makes a woman feel as if he can see inside her soul. If something is bothering you, you'll never need to say it because the Cancer can always tell, and he'll immediately let you know that he cares.

The Cancer man is also incapable of judging others. He wants people to know that they are accepted exactly as they are, because deep down, that's what he wants from you. I know a Cancer man whose ability to give comfort and support made women, including wives of friends and women thirty years his senior, fall hard for him. Of course, he's always shocked when women confess they're in love with him because that is never his intention. It's not that he seeks to attract these women; it's just that he hates to see anybody in pain. His kindness comes off as interest or availability.

Cancer has a hard time hurting anybody's feelings, so he often makes it worse by keeping quiet about how he simply wants to be a friend. If he gets paired with the least attractive girl in a group, he will spend the evening making sure she feels like the most beautiful, desirable female in the bar.

Like a good mother, he has the ability to see a woman's deepest desire and make it come true.

Cancer needs to take care of people and to nurture and support them, especially through a crisis. He can sometimes give so much that he leaves little for himself and winds up getting burnt out. In a relationship, he wants a woman who he can merge with mind, body and soul. If he picks the wrong woman, Cancer will fall into the darkest depression, and it may take years for him to awake from the nightmare.

The Crab is ruled by the moon, and therefore is very sensitive and moody. If you're looking for an Alpha male who will beat his chest and toot his own horn all the while staying on the surface about his feelings, then you need to sidestep the Cancer. This is a deeply emotional man who has the bleeding heart of Mother Teresa and has no problem telling you all about his feelings. It doesn't matter how tough he appears on the surface because underneath is a sensitive romantic who wants your approval.

Remember that the symbol for the Cancer is the crab, a hard-shelled crustacean with an inner softness. When you think of the Cancer man, I bet that Mike Tyson and 50 Cent don't come to mind. They are both hard on the outside, but if you listen to any interview, you'll detect their softer inner side. No matter how hard they work to cover up their vulnerability, it'll come through. Both were motherless at an early age, which is toughest on a water child, who needs to be able to be soft. This could account for the hard Cancer shell they cover themselves with to come across as Alpha males.

The Crab rarely opens up, so when he gets disappointed or hurt, he'll retreat back inside his shell, refusing to open up again. It can take years before he'll open up and trust another person. The worst thing is to meet a Crab after he's been romantically injured. If you have any kind of heart, you'll want to love the pain away because he'll usually go into vivid details describing the bad breakup. Even when he was the cause of the breakup, he'll come across as so sorry or vulnerable that you'll want to do anything to make him feel better.

And while you're listening to his tale of woe, you'll find yourself seduced into wanting to be the woman who won't hurt or disappoint him.

Unfortunately, you might be waiting in the wings for years before his heart shows any sign of availability. Believe me when I tell you that there are women waiting for their phones to ring with a call from a Cancer man, wishing he was available and interested in them.

In relationships, the Cancer needs to be adored and understood. As a moon child, he is at the whim of his emotions, often allowing them to spill wherever, whenever they appear. He can't contain the avalanche of feelings constantly welling up inside of him. The Cancer man can come across as clingy, but that means he's into you. He wants his woman to be part best friend, part confidant, part therapist, part mother and part sex machine.

He is a stable person and usually has his finances together. When it comes to making money, the Cancer is a solid earner. He is also great at saving money. He likes quality, but he's not one to waste money on clothes. The Cancer does have a weakness for travel and likes to go first class. His passport usually has lots of miles on it, and he's always ready to go.

Unlike the Cancer female, the Cancer man is a lot pickier about who he lets into his bed. Even if the Cancer is calling you three times a day and making you the center of his life, this may not be a sign that he's ready for a relationship. Cancer is not a casual dater. That's not to say he doesn't know how to have fun, but he likes to connect with someone in a deep, meaningful and lasting way. That's why he can't stand letting a woman get close when he knows she is not the one. He can't live with himself if he's hurt a female.

When he does find that special someone, she should consider herself a very lucky woman. In a relationship, the Cancer has no problem being the traditional man and letting the woman be the traditional female. But if you are career driven, he'll support your dreams. Basically, when he's in love, he just wants whatever makes his woman happy.

Cancers enjoy fine dining and fancy food, and will wine and dine a woman exactly as she dreamed when she was a little girl. If you have a shot at this man and you're cool with the emotional changes, then you should go for it, because he'll always make sure you have the life you fantasized about.

Let's Get It Started

If you can show a Cancer man that you're interested in the world, especially helping children, he will give you his full attention. Show him that you are really interested in what he has to say. Since he's a huge talker, this may be a test of your listening skills. He's passionate and funny, and usually doesn't mind that conversations can last for hours. I know a Cancer man who could stay on the telephone for eight hours at a time and never get winded.

Unless he's had a few drinks, most Cancer men like to get to know you a bit before rushing between the sheets. Tell him a bit about yourself. He loves funny, embarrassing stories since he believes that many things only happen to him.

The Cancer man is Mr. Fix-it. Share an issue you're having at work or with a family member. When it comes to dating the Cancer man, you can put all your issues on the table up front. He'll get turned on by how honest you are. He doesn't need his woman to be a complete mystery. If you haven't gotten all your stuff together, then let him know because maybe he has some advice that might help. He feels needed when he is able to give advice to help your other relationships work better.

The Cancer man needs lots of attention, so if you're getting to know him, try to have one-on-one time. He won't appreciate sharing you with a crowd of people, at least not in the beginning.

Show him your warm nurturing side. He won't be interested in a woman who seems cold or indifferent. Whatever you do, please don't be blunt with him about his faults because, in spite of his thick-shelled exterior, he's very sensitive. He'll avoid direct confrontations and repeat stories of hurt from years ago.

If he invites you to dinner, chances are it'll be a fancy restaurant, so know how to hold your fork and don't talk with your mouth full. This brother is a complete romantic, so don't have a trash mouth or behave like a pig, or he'll get up and walk away. He likes a woman who is not afraid of her sensuality, so if you've got it, by all means, flaunt it. When he drops you off at home, let him tongue you down. The Cancer likes to know that you're capable of being passionate.

Be patient because the Cancer is super protective of his feelings and keeps his guard up until he trusts you. Go slow because this is not a brother who rushes into relationships until he knows the woman well. But if you're able to wait, this relationship will be well worth it.

Keeping Him Happy

- Cook him romantic dinners.
- Write poetry or send him the lyrics to his favorite song.
- Always dress like a sexy woman.
- Invite his family over for weekly dinners.
- Compliment him as often as possible.
- Make him laugh.
- Deal with his moods without complaining.
- Take his mother on a vacation with you.
- Don't waste money.
- Play water sports with him.

Sex

When the Cancer man is young, his approach to sex is more romantic. He wants to believe that he is the teacher and you are the student. Cancer can be insecure about his sexual prowess, which is why he prefers you to be less experienced. He'll lead you through the steps, letting you grow comfortable, as if you were a virgin. If you are a virgin, the Cancer is the perfect man to give yourself to.

This is not to say he's a wimp. In fact, he's the opposite between the sheets. He'll be aggressive and take total control of you sexually, but he can also be kind and caring. Cancer is the perfect combination of sensitivity and passion.

He can seem old-fashioned because he likes his woman to be ultra feminine, but he'll also want her to be strong and independent. He's a total contradiction, but on him, it works. When you're getting to know him, practice being lady-like. He likes feminine lingerie, so don't be surprised if this brother has his own Victoria's Secret account and surprises you with gifts. I know a Cancer who went through the catalogue for his girlfriend, marking all the must-haves.

The Crab might be moody about some things, but sex is not one of them, especially as he matures and becomes confident about his abilities in bed. He lives to please his woman. Even in the car, he'll reach over and stimulate your clitoris, bringing you to orgasm during a traffic jam. He'll note your response to whatever you like and he'll pull it out of his bag of tricks when you least expect it. He has the memory of an elephant, so you'll never have to tell him twice what you like. This is a man who loves women, and needs them to love him back.

The Crab is intensely sensual and will use his instincts to drive you crazy with desire. I know a Cancer man who became so popular in college because of his ability to give women head. Even women who didn't like him lined up for his specialty. Cancer won't care if he has to eat you all night long to bring you to orgasm. He's incredibly patient. Lots of brothers wait until later in life to enjoy the act of cunnilingus, but from the first time the Cancer man made a woman come, he's never stopped going down on women.

Cancer likes sex, but he's also a hopeless romantic who craves a deep and meaningful relationship with a woman. For a Cancer man, sex is the doorway into a deep and lasting relationship. A kiss is just a kiss, unless you're a Cancer. Then it's the beginning of a whole lot more. He's in it for the long-term, and considers it his job to please his woman. Take your time and give him the attention he craves, and he'll reward you generously.

Cancer Turn-Ons

- Let him take the lead.
- Kissing: long, deep and slow.
- Sex anywhere but the bed.
- Lacy, feminine underwear.
- Doggie style.
- Nip at his nipples. He likes a little pleasure/pain.
- High heels in bed.
- Lick him between the thighs.
- He'll make you cum with his fingers.
- Compliment his performance.

Moving On Without Drama

Leaving a Cancer isn't easy. If he has decided that you are the one for him, then chances are he's made lifelong plans for you.

Since he loves his parents, that's a good place to lay the foundation for the breakup. Criticize his mother and tell him you don't think much of his father. Develop an allergy to his pet and tell him you never liked his dog in the first place. To really drive the point home that you're not interested in long-term plans with him, tell him you don't ever want to have children because you don't like them.

Remember that Cancer is highly sensitive and can be needy. He's also very concerned with your opinion of him. Stop giving him compliments, especially after he's gone out of his way to look good. When he offers to take you out to your favorite expensive restaurant, tell him you've lost your appetite and would rather go to McDonald's. If he wants to sit on the couch and cuddle, explain that it's too hot and you need some space.

If none of these suggestions are working, it's time to become completely insensitive. Let him know you're not interested in his feelings or anybody else's, then turn up the volume on your soap opera. After a while, he'll call you on your insensitivity. That's when you should complain that you want a more masculine man, and you're not into all this emotional stuff.

Start to make lots of social plans out of the house, away from him. Stop eating dinner together, and show no interest in spending time with him. Cancers love everything traditional. Without any true stability and a woman with no emotional depth, the Cancer man will be ready to move on. But even then, he won't want to hurt your feelings. He won't confront you and tell you what a horrible girlfriend you've been. He'll slip out quietly. One day, you'll just wake up and he'll be gone.

Compatibility

CANCER

Cancer Man/Aries Woman

He's sensitive, she's blunt. He's fluid, she's swift. So you might ask, how's the sex? If it's preceded by a feud of some sort, it will be hot and steamy. If you're up for an argument, plan on a passion-filled after party.

The Cancer man and the Aries woman do complement each other in different ways outside of the bedroom. Aries is the first sign of the zodiac, so she's like a big sister to everyone, and Cancer behaves like everybody's mother. Aries should keep in mind that Cancer's masculine side can be less physical and more intellectual.

Sex can be good, especially since Cancer has a true dark side and Aries will do anything to please her man. Of course, after the deed is done, Aries is ready to go while Cancer prefers to cuddle. His sex is a way to express his inner feelings, so Aries's "hit it and quit it" approach will not work.

When Aries songbird, Mariah Carey dated Cancer baseball superstar Derek Jeter, it didn't take a psychic to figure out that this would not work. A Cancer man needs a calm, nurturing presence, and the Aries woman always comes first, which means the Cancer man feels neglected and gets his feelings hurt. He retreats into his shell, and she's off holding court for a throng of admirers. This is not a match that can last for very long.

Cancer Man/Taurus Woman

These two have similar desires. Mr. Cancer gives her security she wants, and Ms. Taurus gives him a place to feel safe and sexy. Cancer and Taurus are both homebodies who prefer to have luxurious dinners in the home. Cancer needs a woman who likes being feminine, and Taurus loves any reason to shop for a slinky new dress.

Mr. Cancer will enjoy exploring and nurturing her body. Sex between the two is soft, lustful, enjoyable, meaningful and hot. It could give a whole new meaning to the word passion. He will give her the sexual attention she craves, and she will give him the calm stability he needs. They are affectionate, and would not have a problem if they decided to spend their lives together. This could definitely go long-term.

Cancer Man/Gemini Woman

As sex goes, this duo would have a good affair. These two have a strong attraction. They will have imaginative sexual ideas that they are game to try. Gemini will readily experience her sexual fantasies with her Cancer partner, which will include bondage and sadomasochism. He will initially enjoy the variety, but if he feels it is not rooted in emotion, he will eventually become turned off.

Cancer wants sex to lead to a deeply satisfying connection with another human being, but to the Gemini, sex is like a competitive sport, and she wants to see how far she can push herself.

In the back of Cancer's mind is the fact that Ms. Gemini can be flighty, and this will not give him the security he needs. Gemini tends to be a bit of a playa, and to the Cancer man, that will only wound his sensitive ego.

Passion will definitely be a part of this sexual duo, but beyond that, it might be just a bit too much work.

Cancer Man/Cancer Woman

Imagine two people who are just content in the privacy of their home. This duo loves to connect emotionally, and looks for the deeper meaning when having sex. They should try sex outdoors, the beach, poolside, or somewhere near the water.

Since neither of them enjoys confrontation, there will probably be more silent treatment than screaming. This combo is usually not interested in a fling or short-term relationship, but making it for the long term can be challenging. The Cancer female needs an Alpha male, while the Cancer male needs an Alpha female in order to have the balance that they crave.

For a while, they will talk about their feelings and be seduced into thinking that their relationship can work. But Cancers need someone to need them, and with these two clinging to each other all day long, they will get nothing done. This pairing is too emotional to survive.

Cancer Man/Leo Woman

The good news is that these two can have wonderful, creative sex. Leo likes to be in control, and Cancer will not have a problem letting the Leo female get on top and ride all day. The bad news is that after the sex, they'll realize how different the experience was for each of them. He needs the sex to be more than an exercise, but for the Leo, she doesn't need every connection to be deep and meaningful.

Cancer will give Leo the attention she craves. He will most likely find he is the one who has to make most of the compromises in the relationship because Leo is into power and control and needs to run things. Cancer won't let that deter him, though. If he has invested time and energy in this union and his heart is in it, he will find a way to make it work.

Even if Leo doesn't tell Cancer how much she feels for him, the fact that she allows him to be her man means that she's right there with him. She does appreciate his passionate and sensitive lovemaking, and finds comfort and security in him. Although they are not a match made in heaven, both like to be in love and need it in order to feel happy. This relationship has a fifty/fifty chance of working out.

Cancer Man/Virgo Woman

These two are a respectful couple. Sex will most likely not set off an explosion, but it is filled with emotion. She will feel nurtured the way she likes, but she should watch her tongue. If Cancer feels she's criticizing him, he will shut off emotionally, and the desire for sex goes out the window.

These two can enjoy simple sex or nasty sex, but it all depends on how safe the Virgo feels with the Cancer man. He will like the way she takes care of him and doesn't spend all his money, but she'll have a problem with his need for luxury.

When the relationship loses it passion, these two know how to stay in synch. With Cancer's needs to feel connected and Virgo being one of the most faithful signs, these two can relish in the fact that together, they will not need to cheat.

This relationship is one of the old-fashioned unions.

Great sex might become good sex, then minimal sex, but if they ride that rollercoaster, they will have something solid and lasting.

Cancer Man/Libra Woman

These are two hopelessly romantic people. Put them in a cozy room, preferably their bedroom, with sexy music and a soft bed, and it's going to be a magical night. Cancer usually prefers the comforts of a one-on-one relationship, while Libra likes to be the social butterfly. But if they spot each other from across the room, they can pick up each other's sexual vibe.

Libra shoudn't read too much into Cancer's sentimental nature. It is what it is. She should just pucker up and get ready for lots of kissing— and I'm not talking about only on the lips.

These two love luxury and travel. Together, they'll enjoy intimate dinners and lots of five-star vacations. However, these things can only sustain a relationship for so long. Cancer wants a soul connection, and in the long run, it might be more than Libra can deliver. In the end, they want two different things from a relationship. They should try staying in the bedroom as often as possible. That way, they will be able to enjoy the party for as long as it lasts.

Cancer Man/Scorpio Woman

Of the two, Cancer is the more conservative sex partner, but Scorpio can set a lovemaking vibe that will have Cancer letting go and getting wild. There might be a few tears shed during their sexual encounter because their lovemaking can be a deeply spiritual experience, fulfilling dreams neither thought were possible. Since these two are water signs, their emotions tend to run deep.

Each can be quite moody, but they handle their moodiness in different ways, with Scorpio shutting down and Cancer brooding. If they value the relationship, they will trust each other and stay open instead of being punishing.

When Cancer gets busy, Scorpio will feel neglected and torture him with the steady stream of men waiting to take his place. Cancer will see right through Scorpio's game and instead of fighting, he will comfort her and make her give up the need to be in control. Scorpio has a dark side, so Cancer should beware. He might find himself under her spell and do whatever it takes to keep her sexiness at his side. This is a relationship that could take some serious work if the couple wants to stay together long-term.

Cancer Man/Sagittarius Woman

"Should I stay, or should I go?" That is the question a Sagittarian will ask herself when she is involved with a Cancer man. An emotional tug of war between these two is a given. Sagittarius loves to feel free, out in the world, and Cancer would rather make a comfortable, stable home for his family with his woman at his side at all times.

Once Cancer has his dream woman, he won't feel the need for anything else, but Sag always needs to be surrounded by people. Cancer's need for consistency and depth will clash with Sag's need to keep things spontaneous and light. He will want to be her entire world, but the Sagittarius isn't giving that honor to a mere mortal. She needs freedom, and the Cancer's clingy love will eventually feel like a prison cell.

While dating, a Sagittarian might find herself flourishing sexually and exploring new dimensions, and Cancer will enjoy a level of sex that takes him into a whole new world. These two like to put their devilish fantasies on the table and play them out.

Cancer must remember that just because sex is great and feels like it could lead to something more permanent, it might not be the same for Sagittarius. Sex for her would likely be an opportunity to play a little before she's in the wind again. Let's call this what it is: sex with no benefits.

Cancer Man/Capricorn Woman

These two are opposites. They are both categorized as homebodies, but in very different ways. Cap's home is a place she goes to as a retreat from work. Mr. Cancer's home is warm and nurturing, a place he prefers to the drudgery of work.

Both are into their families and will want to spend lots of time in their company. Cancer has a bleeding heart and attracts lots of dead beats begging for handouts, but to the Capricorn, that is criminal. She works too hard for her money, and loving Cancer means she works hard for his, so she won't stand for it being given out freely.

In the sack, sex might be compelling, perhaps dutiful, or rough, but nonetheless nurturing. Capricorn must know that her Cancer mate will desire affection, but he'll never ask for it. A Capricorn woman will trust the Cancer male, which will allow her to open up to him and be more affectionate than normal, and the Cancer will understand what it takes to help his Cap partner open up. These two want the same things: love, family and a healthy bank balance. They have a good chance at thriving in a long-term relationship.

Cancer Man/Aquarius Woman

Okay, let's start with the sex. It will be fabulous. These two are different, but that won't matter when they are between the sheets. Aquarius woman is a freak when it comes to sex, and the Cancer man is always up to a challenge

When she lets loose on Cancer, he will never want to leave the bedroom. Cancer is filled with emotions and can be clingy. Aquarius, on the other hand, needs space in order to go out into the world and make a difference. She likes variety and enjoys being spontaneous, while Cancer is conservative and likes to play by the rules.

Cancer wants a traditional female who likes being a wife and mother, and the Aquarius isn't sure she wants children until she actually has them. It's important for both of them to make a difference in this world, but they go about it differently. In the end, neither will be satisfied trying to fit into the other's world.

Cancer Man/Pisces Woman

This is a soul connection with incredible sexual energy. Both are water signs, which makes them emotional creatures who need to have a spiritual union in order to be fulfilled. They are two deep individuals who bring their emotions together to create a great relationship outside of the bedroom.

They have no problem expressing their feelings or being affectionate toward one another.

Neither is afraid to be clingy or needy, since that's who they really are. A sexy duo that marches to their own beat, they can stay alone forever and never need others.

You will see sparks flying when these two get busy. Domestic harmony? Yes, that too, along with intense multiple orgasms. Mr. Cancer will be happy that he has finally found a woman who understand him and doesn't complain about his moods.

If Ms. Pisces is looking for a relationship that has the potential to go beyond sex, she should stop looking when she finds a Cancer man.

Famous Cancer Men

JUNE 22–JULY 22

50 Cent—July 6, 1975
Derek Jeter—June 26, 1974
Forest Whitaker—July 15, 1961
Mike Tyson—June 30, 1966
Bill Cosby—July 12, 1937
Kadeem Hardison—July 14, 1965
Allen Payne—July 7, 1968
Eddie Griffin—July 15, 1968
Chiwetel Ejiofor—July 10, 1974
Henry Simmons—July 1, 1970

Leo

July 23–August 22

Your Leo Man

The Lion is a proud, strong, fearless leader who expects everyone to worship him. And why shouldn't he? After all, the Leo male is king of his world, and you should feel honored to even be invited to the party. What you might not know is that for the Leo, every day is an opportunity to party.

This is an outgoing sign, so much so that the party doesn't start until the Leo shows up. If you really want to make it fun, then go ahead and throw the party in his honor. There is nothing subtle about this sign. Everything about him is up front and intended to get your attention. A good time for the Leo is whenever he can be admired and doted on by everyone around him. Women crave him, and men want to be him when they grow up. He's a magnet for any women who come within his reach.

An easy way to picture the beautiful Lion primping in front of his subjects is to think of

Wesley Snipes and Isaiah Washington, both Leos. They are always well turned out, and they stand as if they expect crowds of people to come to them. Now think of Leo Senator Barack Obama running for President of the United States. Most Washington newcomers wouldn't have the guts to run for a presidential nomination, but Barack, as a Leo, has the hubris necessary to tackle such a feat. More than a few superstar athletes, actors and singers have been born under the Leo sign, which makes sense because not only do Leos like to be the center of everyone's attention; they're usually charismatic and talented.

To the Leo man, romantic love is as important as breathing, which is why he keeps a steady stream of girlfriends. This brother loves to be in love, but the hard work required to achieve a deeper level of connection doesn't always interest them.

When you meet the Leo male, he is usually somewhere between falling in love and falling out of love. He needs a woman in order to fully feel like a man. And you should know that he wants his woman to serve him and to make his life easier. He's not looking for an independent Alpha girl; he wants a soft, feminine, girly girl to dote on him. He has a set of do's and don'ts for anyone who wants to be close to him.

This Lion is one of the most generous and giving signs in the zodiac. Think of him as the king who wants to make sure his subjects have all their needs met so they can go back to the important business of worshipping him. He can be stern with the people closest to him. He expects them to be perfect and to never let him down.

Yes, it's a large order, but he'll inform you that he's worth it. Leo is the brother to write you a check when you're in danger of being evicted. Just don't ask him to drive you home because your car got impounded. He doesn't usually pass judgment on people he loves who are down on their luck, but there is a limit to how close he wants to be to anybody's problems.

One of the major reasons that Leo is so generous is that he likes it when people owe him. You can accept the gifts and favors if you like, but remember that old saying, "There is no such thing as free lunch." A Lion will keep score of everything he's given to you versus everything that you've given to him, and one day he expects those numbers to even out in his favor. If the Leo is more financially successful than you can ever imagine, then instead of money, he will barter for your time. He'll expect your full attention whenever and wherever he wants, and believe me when I say it will be often.

Leo famously takes care of everyone in his family because he has a Midas touch when it comes to making money. Everything he touches seems to turn to gold, but he has to work hard to save, since it's not in his nature. Leo forgets to put aside a little something for a rainy day because when the money is flowing, it's difficult to imagine it will ever stop.

When it comes to fashion, Leo is ahead of the crowd. He often starts a fashion trend two years ahead of the pack. He loves to be copied and believe the old adage that imitation is the sincerest form of flattery. Of course, Leo would never copy anyone else's look.

In a relationship, the Leo man needs a woman he can respect, or else he'll kick her to the curb. If he suspects she's cheating, he'll move on to a new Ms. Right and never look back. Leo can handle a lot of issues from his woman, as long it doesn't include another man. This expectation of fidelity doesn't go both ways, though. The Leo man needs constant attention, and he won't see anything wrong from getting it from other women. I know a Leo man who cheated on his girlfriend so much that his friends thought he'd have to marry her in order to keep her.

He is extremely self-involved, but he can't help himself; he's his biggest fan. If the Leo man is going through heartbreak or an earache, he'll forget anyone else exists except himself. Of course, after he's done licking his wounds, he's ready to be fabulous again.

The Leo is often disappointed by his subjects, but never in himself. He feels he is perfect, and can't begin to see any flaws in his personality. No matter how he contributed to the failure of a job or relationship, it is never, ever his fault. If you try to make a Leo brother take responsibility for any of your relationship issues, it'll be a long and futile fight. He hates to be wrong, and more than that, he can't stand being seen as imperfect in any way. He'll fight to the death to preserve the vision he has of himself, so be careful when the gloves come off.

Leo is a sensitive soul, but he's not the type to wear his feelings on his sleeve. He rarely lets anyone see how he really feels, but if you look closely, you'll notice the chink in the armor he shields himself in.

Leo could use some help learning to be gracious. When you go out of your way to do something special for a Lion he'll immediately forget a simple "thank you." It's partly that he believes everything in the world should be praising him in the first place. As king of the jungle, all the trinkets and gifts he receives from his subjects, including you, are his birthright.

The Lion likes to order people around and tell them how to live their lives. He'll give the best advice—even if you notice he won't take it himself. He'll demand you stop going into debt by making frivolous purchases, and the next time you see him, he'll be rocking all the latest gear, even though he's between jobs. Think of him as the supreme ruler who dictates to his subjects the best way to get their lives in order. Just don't ever expect him to follow his own advice.

If you're the type of woman who doesn't mind being a trophy wife, the wind beneath his wings, or living in his shadow, a relationship with a Leo can be fulfilling.

Let's Get It Started

Getting the Lion's attention is one of the easiest things in the world to do. Give him compliments and tell him what you admire about him. Just remember that he is used to women trying to impress him, so your method has to be different to make you stand out from all the others. While they are fawning all over him, you have to stay laid back. Let them be the ones who look like they're trying too hard. Make your compliments more subtle and intriguing. While the other women are complimenting him on the obvious things, he'll be impressed when you comment on little details that show you're paying close attention. He'll appreciate that you noticed those new cufflinks while everyone else couldn't get past that old, tired line about his sexy eyes. Try to add a little humor to your approach too. He likes a woman who can make him laugh, and that usually leads to something more.

I knew a Leo man who worked out every day and wore tight shirts to show off his guns. Women couldn't help but drool over his body, but he refused to give a woman a second date if she complimented him on his biceps. The woman he married admired his business sense and all his ideas about making the world work better. So, if you run up on a Lion and want to impress him, try the less obvious route.

On a first date, put your best foot forward. Wear your best dress, get waxed and make sure your hair is right. Leo likes it when his woman looks good, because it brings even more attention his way if all eyes are on you as a couple.

He will most likely take you to an upscale social event. Leos love to hang out with the popular crowd, so you can expect to visit some of the hottest clubs with your Leo. Ignore the other men in the room and keep your attention on him. He'll notice this and reward you later.

In a relationship, you will gain brownie points by singing his praises about the way he knows how to satisfy a woman. He loves to know that you have told your friends how great he is both in and out of bed. But be careful because he won't throw those girlfriends out if they ask for a sample of that Lion action in the bedroom.

Keeping Him Happy

- Leos need luxury, so bring champagne over.
- Always treat him like the king he is.
- Stroke his ego; it's huge.
- Be charming and outgoing.
- Always remind him that he is the most important person in your life.
- Make him laugh.
- Keep it fabulous. Be extravagant.
- Dress to impress.

Sex

When it comes to sex, like everything else, the Leo man expects to have whatever he wants. He also wants you to do most of the work because after all, he is king of the jungle. It's your job to turn him on, and once you get him going, you better deliver. Leo can't stand women who brag about their ability to perform and then disappoint.

Because he believes he is all that, Leo doesn't always work to get compliments in the bedroom. This doesn't mean that you'll never experience an orgasm with a Leo. It's just that when it comes to sex, the Lion is all about the two of you pleasing him. What? You thought you would ever be enough for the Lion?

Unfortunately, the Leo is likely to skip right over foreplay and tell you to get down on your knees and worship the royal penis. Maybe I'm being harsh, but you might have to tell him to stop pushing your head into his crotch. He can't seem to help it; he's concerned about having his needs met.

When it comes to intercourse, he'll ride you like a stallion. And since he's usually strong, he'll flip you over like a rag doll. No matter his age, the Leo has the stamina of a twenty-year-old and will wear you out long before he's done. He likes to be in control during sex, so put on your most passive face and let him have total control. If he's into S&M, then you are the submissive and he is the master. Don't be surprised if he whips out the handcuffs and leather outfit to drive home his need to totally dominate.

Leo is turned on by viewing his image as he penetrates you, so remember, lights on. More than a few Leos have gotten caught on tape because they like to play back their sex scenes.

This is a man who needs to be turned out in order to like a woman enough to stay interested. If you're lukewarm about the Leo, don't worry. There are always a slew of women waiting to take your place. But if you're turned on by a dominant man and don't mind doing what it takes to keep him, then go for it. Let him maintain sexual control, and your Leo will learn to worship you.

Leo Turn-Ons

- Take him to a sex shop.
- Model your skimpiest lingerie.
- Suck him until he cums.
- Handcuff him to the bed and go down on him.
- Be open to role reversal.
- Let him start out with the control and then flip the script.
- Big tits, especially if they're fake.
- Flattery and compliments.
- Be his sex slave.

Moving On Without Drama

The first thing you have to know is that nobody leaves a Leo. The best way to get out of a relationship with a Leo is to let him leave you. This doesn't take much work. In fact, just stop working so hard to worship him, and he'll be gone in a hurry.

Stop paying him the excessive attention he needs. If he starts to tell you a story about himself (his favorite subject) take out your phone and start scrolling through your texts while he's talking. Interrupt him and tell him that you need to respond to a text immediately. When you're finished, don't bother to ask him to finish his story. Make sure he gets the message that you weren't really interested in the first place.

Instead of listening to him, spend plenty of time talking about yourself. Focus on serious topics only. Talk constantly about problems at work. Act like your issues are so important that you have no time left for him. If you do tell him a joke, make it a corny one. It will drive him crazy to be with a woman who has lost her sense of humor.

Spend lots of time in front of the television, and turn up the volume whenever he starts talking to you. When he asks you to attend another social function with him, tell him you can't go out that night because you don't want to miss the latest Lifetime movie. On the night of the event, go into the bedroom while he's getting dressed and criticize whatever he is wearing. If you're really not afraid of danger, tell him his suit makes him look fat.

Basically, if the Leo male thinks you're putting anything else before his needs, he'll be through with you. Just don't let him think it's another male who's making you act this way. Leo is competitive, and he won't stand for being left for another man. If you're cheating, you better get away before he finds out, or else you'll have to deal with that Leo wrath.

You won't have to worry about closure after breaking up with Mr. Leo. When he's done with you, trust that he is completely done. Once you dare to disrespect this king, he'll change his phone number, block all your calls and move on without a backward glance.

Compatibility

LEO

Leo Man/Aries Woman

Sex, love, it's all good here. This is a hot, fiery combination. The Leo man likes to be king of the jungle, and the Aries woman insists on coming first. While this might be a problem in other relationships, these two make it work. Aries is able to let Leo hold center court as long as he isn't trying to date other women. And she gives him reason to stay faithful. He needs to be stimulated, and the Aries woman provides plenty of excitement for him.

Both love to be on the go and in the middle of whatever is happening. When passion calls their names, they answer, each willing to drive the other crazy with desire. Expect a boatload of role-playing and creative positioning and pure carnal pleasure. He likes to receive oral sex and she loves to give it, and doesn't seem to care if she's never on the receiving end.

There will be no holding back when it comes to their emotions because both love to be in love, especially if it can be easy and fun. They do have challenges because the Lion isn't good at sharing his spotlight, and occasionally the Aries expects to be the focus of his attention.

They both like the same things, so maybe this can go the distance.

Leo Man/Taurus Woman

This couple is good together in the bedroom. They are both strong-willed, and sex between them will be hot and heavy. They both like to be on top, but Taurus is a lady, so she'll allow her man to do the heavy lifting as long as he springs for the occasional shopping spree. If Taurus wants to keep the sexual passion burning, then she has to remember that famous Leo ego, ego, ego.

Leo loves to be stroked, and not just on his private parts. Taurus must remember to take care of her Leo man's ego because he needs it as much as she needs those new shoes. Leo is generous, and Taurus likes to spend money, which makes for a perfectly material match.

Taurus wants loyalty, and Leo wants to be told he's the greatest thing since sliced bread. Taurus likes to stay at home more than the Leo, who prefers to be on the go wherever the party happens to be. They each need to learn to give in a little more. If they can knock out some of their stubborn behavior, they can get along well.

Leo Man/Gemini Woman

This is a match that's full of laughter, fun and adventure. They can have a great time together in the bedroom. One thing Gemini should know is that Leo loves oral stimulation and prefers to be on the receiving end. He'll go down on her, but when he's done, he'll expect seconds. When things are good between these two, the Leo will reward Gemini with nights filled with passion that knock her wildest fantasy right out of the ballpark.

Problems happen when Gemini wants to be intellectually stimulated and Leo would rather play than sit around watching CNN. Leo might find himself having to deal with Gemini's lack of dependability. She is a twin and can be one of the hardest signs to figure out. She can be smart, funny, and charming, or a sexy beast that he would like to get naked between the sheets with.

Hopefully, things will go well because neither of these signs has the ability to forgive once things have gone wrong. This pair is capable of a one-night stand or a year-long affair, but they should think long and hard before trying to make this permanent.

Leo Man/Cancer Woman

She a lady's lady; he's the man's man. This is a partnership with no long-term prospects that will fizzle as soon as the sensitive Cancer learns that the Leo can be a thoughtless Lion. Cancer is a homebody who wants to take care of a man, make dinner and nest, and Leo is the original rolling stone who doesn't want anything to hold him down.

Sexually, they can have fun for a short while. The Leo loves how sensuous and sexual the Cancer can be when her passion is ignited. Cancer will do anything to please the Lion, and that includes role-playing and bondage. She will enjoy how he loves to show off for her in the bed. All the world is a stage for a Leo man. The more he performs, the more she will feed his desire for affection and adoration.

But Cancer wants to feel that this union is built on more than just sex. She's not the bootiecall type. Both signs need to be in love in order to feel good about themselves, but even the fantasy of togetherness cannot last. Sexually, these two can work, but the relationship will need a miracle in order to grow into more than a fling.

Leo Man/Leo Woman

My sex is better than your sex.

Can we talk egos? Sex will be hot and passionate and often because they both view it as a way to show off their moves. You might find them one-upping each other in the bed. Lovemaking for them might as well be in a theatre where they can sell tickets for an audience to view a late-night performance. These two could go into the adult sex industry together because they each love to be the stars of their own movies. Screaming and yelling at the peak of an orgasm, moans and groans in between, they are the couple most likely to swap couples, as long as they can be watched.

If these two don't learn how to share the spotlight, their competitive bedside fun will eventually wear thin. Besides, how many Leos can you take in one relationship?

Leo Man/Virgo Woman

In the bed, Virgo likes to take her time. She's an old-fashioned kind of girl who plays for keeps. Sex with her and her Leo man will be good, as long as she's checked him out and is comfortable about his character. Whatever she decides to play along with—French maid, or a damsel in distress—she will only want to role-play for her long-term mate. Leo's sexual ability will make her heart skip a beat and fill the room with sparks.

Leo will have to learn to deal with Virgo's need for perfection, which comes with a steady helping of criticism. She's classy and puts herself together with care, and expects the same from her mate. The irony is that Leo also has a need for perfection, and can be hypercritical. This will be a tough hurdle for them to overcome.

Leo likes to hang out and take it as it comes, but the Virgo wants an itinerary detailing all his moves. She'll never stand for his social calendar; there is too much to accomplish in this lifetime to run the streets. The only way this relationship will be a love affair is if neither expects it to last longer than a week.

Leo Man/Libra Woman

Sex in public places is definitely on top of the to-do list for this couple. Libra woman pretends to be Miss Goody-two-shoes, but behind closed doors, she's all freak. In the bedroom, they have lots in common because they're both down for whatever. They complement each other because both love the game of sex.

She will be turned on by the Leo's overt sexuality. When another woman comes on to Leo, Libra will watch, and as long as it doesn't go too far, she'll be into it. The competition turns her on. Leo can expect a night of hot sex afterwards.

With Libra, Leo gets to be his fun, outgoing self and nobody asks him where he's been.

You've got a good match here.

Leo Man/Scorpio Woman

"If I were the king of the forest . . ." And Leo thinks he is. But Scorpio sees herself as a queen, so where does that leave this duo? Let's just say sex is exciting, but each person will get the sense that it's all about the other person. This doesn't sit well with these egotistical signs.

These two will relish in each other's sexiness. When in synch, they are sexually off the charts and will need to work out to keep up their stamina.

Scorpio is up for sex anytime she can get it, and she won't care that Leo wants it dirty. But Leo is often out being adored by his public, which means she won't get it as often as she wants. A Scorpio woman is not interested in sharing her man with anybody. After all, she is the most sensuous woman in the zodiac. If she catches him cheating or even just flirting, she will close up shop and put him on sexual punishment.

They complement each other when in the bedroom, but outside in the real world, they just do not make sense. Maybe if they put a lock on their bedroom door . . .

Leo Man/Sagittarius Woman

Fun and fireworks are inevitable with this couple. They are secure enough with each other, both in and out of the bedroom, to let go. Sex will be physical and will involve lots of toys and outside locations. They will begin in the 69 position and take it to new heights on airplanes, balloon rides, and even bungee jumping. New ideas are bountiful with this duo.

Leo will gloat from the many compliments she pays him for her sexual pleasure. He will repay her with showers of affection. She will let him take the lead in bed and expect him to turn up the volume to crazy when he does. Once these two fires signs get started, they can expect to get busy several times a day.

Long-term and marriage are in the cards for this couple because both are secure and can let the other have plenty of breathing space. So, if Leo is looking for Mrs. Right, he has found her. He can get out that tux and Sag . . . well, she knows the rest.

Leo Man/Capricorn Woman

How can great sex happen with this duo? Well, they'll have to be up for a good challenge. Leo's ego won't survive workaholic Capricorn; nor will sensible Capricorn be able to deal with flighty Leo's constant desire for attention and compliments. How can he get her to stroke it— ego, that is—when she's always busy? She puts her spare time to use with her family, definitely not making sure he feels adored.

In the bedroom, Capricorn is practical. If she trusts her partner, she'll be freak of the week, but if she doesn't, she'll go standard missionary and never let him see her wild side. If she does let loose, she can go neck and neck with him in the bed, and she won't need the trumpets blasting

and confetti falling over her to get her in a passionate mood. Leo, on the other hand, wouldn't
mind if an orchestra played a symphony prelude.
Unfortunately for Leo, sexual compliments will
be few and far between—unless, of course, he
pays them to himself, which is not all that far-
fetched.

So basically, there'll be a few moans, but outside of the bedroom, you're likely to hear more
yelling and screaming, and it won't be connected
to the ultimate climax. These two can't make
it past the weekend, but hopefully they'll get a
good night out of it.

Leo Man/Aquarius Woman

Leo feels like the king on the throne with this
Aquarius woman. Aquarius flatters the Leo man
with much attention, which makes it easy for
him to fall for her.

They both like sex and have no problems
when it comes to the bedroom. Sex is an adventure with her; freaky and wild. Lights, camera,
action! An evening of passionate lovemaking
or naughty bondage is sure to get captured on a
Sony mini-cam with this freaky couple. It might
replace the Blockbuster movie they rented and
serve as the feature film selection for a night or
two . . . or three.

She's a loner, not concerned with outside influences, and she desires to change the world.
He's a bit of a narcissist who wants the world
to be a better place for him. Once these two can
come to a meeting of the minds, they could have
a chance for the long-haul.

Leo Man/Pisces Woman

There will be an immediate attraction when
these two meet, but it could go downhill from
there. Leo will run all over this sensitive woman,
especially when she gets emotionally involved.

Pisces likes to please the man she is with, so
she'll do whatever he wants her to do. This will
lead to unbelievable sex that alters their whole
being. The Pisces woman will find the Leo's
strong sexuality attractive. His sexual passion
and enthusiasm will all but make up for his lack
of creativity.

Pisces is capable of helping the Leo go deep.
But like the water and fire signs they are, once
these two elements mix, there will be nothing
but hot steam, and we know steam will eventually evaporate. She will feel overshadowed by
his domineering personality and realize she has
bitten off more than she can chew. Once Pisces

comes to this realization, she should call it a night. Adiós. Ciao, baby. See ya, wouldn't wanna be ya. You get the idea.

Famous Leo Men

JULY 23–AUGUST 22

Fat Joe—August 19, 1970
Marlon Wayans—July 23, 1972
Kadeem Hardison—July 27, 1965
Laurence Fishburn—July 30, 1961
Wesley Snipes—July 31, 1962
Coolio—August 1, 1963
Michael Ealy—August 3, 1973
Isaiah Washington—August 3, 1963
Marques Houston—August 4, 1981
Kool Moe Dee—August 8, 1962
Kurtis Blow—August 9, 1953
Michael Bivens—August 10, 1968
Lil' Romeo—August 19, 1989
Isaac Hayes—August 20, 1942

Virgo

August 23–September 22

Your Virgo Man

First, the good news is this: If you have lucked up on a Virgo man, you are about to consider yourself blessed. He is a strong, determined and passionate man who will go out of his way to make you feel loved. On the flip side, he can be hypercritical and pick you apart like a chicken bone.

The Virgo man is rarely casual about anything, especially his heart. You can bet that before the Virgo pursues a relationship, he has graduated from Relationship 101 with honors. He's read all the relationship books, questioned couples who have been successfully married for years, and studied the issues and habits most likely to end in divorce.

He's not looking for a one-night stand unless he's been recently wounded by love. What he longs for is his life partner, someone who shares similar views and desires, and he realizes that in order to have that, he must enter a relationship through the door of friendship.

Virgo likes to know the woman he gets involved with very well. In fact, he might take so much time that you will be tempted to toss him into the friend zone and write him off as an acquaintance just as he's starting to look at you as a viable life partner.

Part of the reason Virgo is so careful about entering into a relationship is he does not like to fail at anything. Even though he comes across as a cool brother, underneath, he's wrestling with his insecurity, which is why he needs everything in his life to be perfect. No matter how things are going, he has already scheduled a back-up plan. This man's motto is "If you fail to plan, then you plan to fail."

This tendency to plan everything crosses over into his work life too. Virgo has a very strong work ethic. When he is in work mode, which is often, it's hard to get him thinking about romance or love. He's the kind of man who keeps his schedule updated daily and has a backup calendar in case modern technology fails, and he doesn't deal well with being asked to change his plans. Some women will find this lack of spontaneity a small price to pay, though, for having a man who is so concerned with her well-being and her future. Virgo loves to provide for his family and make sure that they are financially set.

Virgo wants to be the head of his family. He's a very traditional brother who likes women who are feminine and domesticated. Sometimes his expectations for a woman can be a tall order. His idea of the perfect woman is Halle Berry crossed with Oprah and B. Smith. If you have a Virgo male friend who is single, do yourself a favor and don't bother to set him up on a date. Mr. Virgo will find something wrong with all your choices.

He can be just as picky and demanding even after he's chosen a mate. His mind is like a computer. He'll keep a running tab of all the nice things you've ever said and done for him, but he'll also keep track of anything that he considers negative, including how many times you showed up late. This is a brother who hates his time being wasted.

Virgo is extremely close to his family, so if you have a problem spending holidays with his relatives, this is not the man for you. Virgo vacations with his family, parties with his family, and is often in the family business. There will be impromptu family visits and late-night phone calls. He is the family member that others come to when they are in need. Virgo is the sign of service, and he likes to help those less fortunate than himself.

Because Virgo keeps his own life very structured, he is consumed with other people's lives,
and loves to gossip. He is up on the activities
of all the people in his life, and you will be too.
Suddenly, the normal family and friends you've
met become cast members in a soap opera. And
like it or not, when you are not around, the most
intimate details of your life are shared with his
friends and family. He simply cannot help wanting to keep those close to him informed. It's just
one more way he can feel like he's keeping everything in his life in order.

But in spite of this, if he takes a chance on
you, you could not ask for a better partner. He'll
make sure you have a structured and orderly life.
He has a lot of dreams to make come true, and
that takes a lot of focus, so he won't risk failure
by taking chances. Virgo will make sure that the
woman he loves has a secure and comfortable
future.

Let's Get It Started

Virgo men like smart women. If you speak Ebonics, I'm going to save you some time. This is not the brother for you. Now, if you have a little knowledge and know how to string together a sentence, then by all means, try to get this brother's attention. In fact, brains are a bigger aphrodisiac than the booty to this brother. You can be street smart or book smart; if you can introduce him to new ways of thinking, he'll be intrigued.

He likes to learn and is into self-improvement, so if you speak another language or come from another country, you're halfway there. Capture his attention with your intelligent conversation, but you must be low-key and subtle when it comes to letting him know you're interested. If you come on too strong, you'll lose him immediately. If you've ever heard the phrase, "I don't want to be a member of any club that will have me," you should know that you can apply it to the Virgo man. He's not easy to open up and trust strangers, and he'll wonder why you're rushing to get close to him.

If you do make it to the next step and he asks you out, it is imperative that you're on time for your date. Virgo likes everything structured and orderly, and he can't stand a woman who isn't punctual.

Virgo is traditional, so he will want to be the one to make the plans. He'll take you someplace that is sensibly priced, with good, solid food. There won't be anything flashy about the place, but the service will be exceptional, and chances are the waiter will know him. He's a creature of habit, so it's probable that he's been there before. Whatever you do, don't complain or tell him you would have preferred a trendy restaurant or nightclub. If you want a second date, just smile and thank him for taking you out.

On the date, you'll learn very little about him, but he'll play an intense game of twenty questions. Virgo is naturally curious about people. If the Virgo brother is prying into your personal business, think of it as foreplay. He wants to make sure you're a good person before he gets in between the sheets with you.

If you're feeling this brother and want to keep him around for a while, your job is to convince him that you are a serious contender. Let him know that you are the type of woman who will not only take care of him, but also the kids and the house, all while keeping your appearance together.

Let him know that you are responsible with your money and not a spendthrift. Virgo likes a woman who is careful with her cash because if the relationship has legs, you'll be merging piles of money, and that means you have to have the same respect for it that he does.

He will want to know that you have an eye toward the future. Share your five-year plan with him. What? You don't have a five-year plan? Then I suggest you create one before he picks you up for the first date. You need to prove your stability when it comes to the Virgo man. He will have no interest in a woman who seems distracted or impractical.

Remember, too, that there is a difference between having a plan for the future and having unrealistic dreams. Don't talk about dreams unless you can back them up with a real plan of action to make them come true. Virgo is not a fan of daydreamers. He saves his respect for doers.

A woman should provide just enough information to assure the Virgo that she is stable, but withhold enough to intrigue him. Don't tell your life story on the first date with him. He likes women who are reserved. In fact, never reveal all your dirty secrets to this man.

Virgo plays for keeps, so he will take his time deciding where your relationship is going. If you're into him, be patient. You'll know that he can envision a future with you once he starts making plans to introduce you to his family.

Keeping Him Happy

- Be punctual.
- Give him a gift certificate for books at Amazon. com.
- Be responsible with your money and keep your credit score high.
- Run a bubble bath with candlelight and soft music.
- Take self-improvement classes.
- Never criticize him, and never complain about his criticism.
- Keep your appearance neat.
- Hire a maid once a week, and don't leave your stuff lying around.
- Be devoted to him.
- Have sex as often as you can.

Sex

Virgo is not a brother who falls into bed immediately, unless you give him a push. The Virgo man is rarely the aggressor when it comes to sex. Instead, he prefers the woman to pursue him. He wants things to be clear so that there is no risk of getting his feelings hurt. When you're ready to get busy with your Virgo man, the best thing to do is to let him know up front that you want him to stay the night, so that he can bring all the proper toiletries, his pajamas and that toothpaste he prefers.

This doesn't mean that he will only sleep with you if the two of you are in a committed relationship. Virgo can have a steady sexual partner and treat it as merely a sexual relationship, void of any emotional connection. He doesn't need to be into someone to have sex; however, he does have to respect her. You must be clean and well-mannered. Virgo cannot have sex with anyone no matter how sexy if he finds her distasteful.

He won't take any crass or sexual conversation outside of the bedroom, nor will he be into public displays of affection. If you need a man who will cuddle with you in the movie theater or play footsie under the table in the restaurant, then look elsewhere. Virgo is a fixed sign, so he won't let you talk him into doing anything he's not comfortable with. Don't try to force him, or he'll run the other way.

Don't be discouraged, though. Even if he won't show his affection in public, when Virgo is into a woman, he will do whatever it takes to please her. He will make sure his partner is fully satisfied. If you want something, he's there to listen to your needs. You'll be surprised how good the sex can be with the conservative Virgo.

Usually, he approaches sex exactly as he approaches life: a slow, studied technique. Before you have sex with a Virgo, there is a chance he'll want to work out all the details. He'll want to discuss what you want versus what he wants, and how the entire thing will go down. But don't sleep on having a planned sex session. It can be highly erotic. You'll be surprised how much you look forward to this event.

The Virgo works very deliberately as he services your needs. You'll feel like he's being graded for a test as he slides down between your legs: open, pull back the lips, two licks this way, one nibble that way. The Virgo learned exactly what works, and he sticks to that script. He's not a very creative sign, so don't expect to be blown away by intercourse with him, but know that he will make sure you get yours. You won't believe that the man eating you to multiple orgasms is the same buttoned-down man you just had dinner with.

Like everything else in his life, sex is an analytical pursuit. He's not ever going to be screwed out of his mind, so if you think you can sex a Virgo into a relationship, you are wasting your time. He has a checklist for mates, and unless you meet his ideal of a perfect partner, it's always going to be about sex. If you're cool with that, then go ahead and work on your Virgo man. If you can get him to loosen up, you'll be pleasantly surprised by how much fun can be had.

Virgo Turn-Ons

- Missionary position.
- A soapy shower for two.
- A clean appearance and proper grooming.
- Let him shave your private parts.
- Soft-core porn.
- Do a striptease.
- A soft, luxurious bed.
- Give him oral pleasure.

Moving On Without Drama

A Virgo man knows how to leave a relationship quickly and without incident because he hates drama. Unfortunately, he is loyal to a fault and likes to give you the benefit of the doubt. A Virgo may hang in a little longer once he's made a commitment. You will have to convince him that he has no choice but to leave you.

He needs both you and your environment to be clean, so stop bathing and shaving your private parts. Let the dust bunnies accumulate under the couch and the dirty dishes pile up in the sink. When he complains about the moldy leftovers in the refrigerator, ask him why it's always your job to keep the house clean.

Of course, his answer will be that he goes to work to provide for you, so the least you can do is keep his home clean. This is when you start complaining about how much he works. Tell him that you think the project he's working on is useless. When he's complaining about his job or how someone wasn't prepared, just shrug your shoulders and say, "So what he's not perfect? That would be boring."

Tell him that you want him to take you out more often, then when he does, insist on going to a loud club you know he hates. He wants you to be ladylike, so while you're at the club, start cursing like a sailor and let him catch you checking out the other brothers. Talk about the hunky guy with the amazing abs (or whatever part of the body your Virgo needs to work on). Go ahead and dance with that guy, and your Virgo might just leave you at the club that very night.

If he puts up with this behavior, you have to pull out the big guns. Start wearing sloppy clothes when you go to Sunday dinner with his family, but take your time getting ready so you'll be late getting there. Brag to his mother about some expensive jewelry you're planning to buy with the money you were supposed to be saving for a rainy day. Try to get him to make out with you at the dinner table in front of his whole family. And to deliver the final blow, share with his family the laundry list of complaints you have about him.

Virgo strives for perfection and believes he's pretty close to it, so once you tear him down and embarrass him in front of his family, he'll be showing you the door. Before you know it, Virgo will be gone; and it will be a long time before he's ready to give his heart to someone else.

Compatibility

VIRGO

Virgo Man/Aries Woman

This is an odd couple, but they can have a little fun before they get turned off.

Aries is sexy and uninhibited and has no problem doing all the dirty things she has in the porno hidden under the bed. She will have to spell out her erotic plans for the Virgo, however, to help him feel comfortable. When Aries whips out her maid's costume with the crotchless fishnet pantyhose, she better hope she has a Virgo who is somewhat evolved. She will definitely have her work cut out for her if she is going to get this buttoned-up Virgo to relax and play along.

The union between these two will probably be short-lived. Virgo will have a hard time with the uninhibited Aries. And Ms. Aries will grow tired of Virgo's analytical ways and criticism, because after all, she loves who she is and sees no reason to change.

Virgo Man/Taurus Woman

This match has great love potential. Sexually, these two will be drawn to each other. Sparks may not fly, but love will happen. She is sensual, and that is a plus for the Virgo man, who loves detail. He will pay attention to every nook and cranny as he canvases her body with pleasurable kisses and gyrations. She will love the way he loves her and feel safe to let down her guard.

To others, this couple is quite predictable. Perhaps they are, but if it works, why fix it? They like to take their time before jumping into things. There is sure to be a long-term union if these two so choose.

Virgo Man/Gemini Woman

Virgo might find it a bit challenging to pin down the free-spirited Gemini. Her fickle nature will get under Virgo's skin. He should remember he is dealing with twins, and unless he's in the mood for a threesome, he may want to rethink the ride he's about to take.

But if Virgo chooses a roll in the sack with a Gemini, sex will be good and clean, if they can reach past the meeting of the minds. Both are highly intelligent, but while Gemini grazes a subject, Virgo goes to great lengths to know what he is talking about.

Oral stimulation is a good way to things started. Gemini enjoys the touch and sensual caressing of the breast. Sexually, Virgo will go along with Gemini's sexual thrill, but if he tries to bring her down to his sexual comfort level, she will head for the hills. Don't look for hot and heavy here. In fact, it's a good idea to keep on looking.

Virgo Man/Cancer Woman

Virgo and Cancer, sitting in a tree, K-I-S-S-I-N-G. Well, you know the rest. They are sexually compatible, but it can take a push to get things rolling because neither is aggressive.

Cancer has a tendency to be shy, and Virgo is usually uncomfortable initiating sex. This puts this duo in an awkward position. But all hope is not lost. Because they are both earthy types, they will find a deep trust between them that allows them to go deeper. Once they have established a safe place for themselves, they will find sexual harmony and go all out to make sure they are both sexually pleased.

A good way for this duo to assure an easier union is to start off as friends.

Virgo Man/Leo Woman

If Virgo doesn't mind that Leo is somewhat of a prima dona and has no problem applauding herself often, then this might work. It won't be easy for these two to get it started, though. Leo likes a manly, macho type of man. She wants to be pursued and taken, and won't stand for any hemming and hawing, which is exactly how the Virgo man operates.

To the Leo, anytime she appears is the perfect time to have sex. Sex feels like more of a sport than a personal connection between two people, but the Virgo needs to feel more connected for anything to become a real relationship. When those sheets are pulled back and these two leave the bedroom, Mr. Virgo will quickly grow tired of all that is required to stroke Ms. Leo's ever-bragging ego and screw all night long. This duo is not expected to go it the long-haul, but stranger things have happened.

Virgo Man/Virgo Woman

Can things be any more perfect? Expectations are high with this couple; however, they are usually in synch. Sex is perfect, even if it is sometimes too well thought out.

Serving one another is something they will love, and don't forget about being served. Regular sex, oral sex, any way you serve it up—each understands what the other needs sexually without uttering a single word. Since their rhythms are lined up, they can count on not having to entice each other into the idea of sex. They will be ready for a romp under the sheets at the same time.

Before this duo moves toward a more stable and long-term relationship, you can bet any relationship details have been put on the table and discussed. They should be ironed out, wrinkle-free and ready to go.

Virgo Man/Libra Woman

The Libra woman will find that her Virgo man is a giving lover. He will suggest many fantasies that she will want to try with him, but would have been too shy to initiate on her own. With her Virgo man, she can go for it, and expect to encounter a night of multiple orgasms.

With Virgo's perfectionist nature, however, Libra might find that he has planned out their entire sexual encounter from head to toe—something along the lines of "two hits to the right, one hit to the left." Okay, that's probably a bit overboard, but still, their approaches to sex might be too different to come to any type of common ground. Libra likes things to be easy and breezy and well, the Virgo needs a lot more control to feel safe. Virgo man shouldn't be surprised if Libra can handle the friendship part better than the sexual relationship. This union is not a likely one.

Virgo Man/Scorpio Woman

He's a little bit country, she's a little bit rock and roll. Sometimes the Scorpio woman will suggest things that are so over the top that the Virgo man will wonder if they're even legal. However, if she can get him to unleash, he will have the kind of sex he fantasizes about.

Her bedroom manner . . . well, she doesn't have manners when it comes to sex. She's ready and rearing to go and try new things, while he is more of the take-our-time, think-it-through type of guy. They are at two different levels when it comes to being free. This can be frustrating for a Scorpio.

On the plus side, Virgo is a faithful partner and won't drive Scorpio crazy with jealousy. She will find a pleasing bedroom partner and a relationship that goes deeper than just sex. If Scorpio is willing to be patient and is prepared to handle his perfectionism, there is hope. This combination might turn out to be the steamy affair both of them have dreamed about or the lasting relationship that they have longed for.

Virgo Man/Sagittarius Woman

Sex will not be one of the reasons this duo goes for a long-term union. They mesh nicely between the sheets, but Sagittarius will most likely lead the way. She'll be ready to rev things up and party the night away in the bedroom, while Virgo may be just the opposite.

Their sexual partnership can be a push-and-pull one. She wants to push him into loosening up and going crazy; he will want to pull her in and slow her down. But if either of them succeeds, there is a chance they'll last longer than that weekend.

Staying together past the weekend will require work on their part. The Virgo man will need to crack that by-the-book shell of his and let the joy of sex in many new places and positions flow.

The Sagittarius woman, on the other hand, will need to take time to enjoy her new and improved man without thinking about where or what she's off to do next.

Virgo Man/Capricorn Woman

Perhaps a match made in heaven. Together, this duo can accomplish anything they put their minds to, and that includes sexing each other up until they've reached the most unbelievable orgasms.

These two have a strong sexual bond. The sex is both mental and physical, and they approach everything they do in life with the same sort of passion. Both are intense doers who don't like to waste time, so they'll have no problem scheduling a get-together. They are workaholics and have plans for how most of their lives will run, even in the bedroom. They will sit together and plan how, why, and where they are going to have sex, and they won't think there's anything strange about it. An evening in the hot tub together is perfect for next Thursday night at eight.

Virgo and Capricorn love spending time with the family and will happily do a sit down dinner with them once a week. A long-lasting relationship filled with lots of love is inevitable.

Virgo Man/Aquarius Woman

These two are quite different. The Virgo man walks his talk, and the Aquarius woman talks and dreams. Both have good intentions, but only one consistently follows through. Virgo can easily get distracted by business or future plans, while Aquarius is not interested in his paint-by-the-numbers way of living. Aquarius loves the calmness of Virgo, and she appreciates his attention to detail, but she needs a little less buttoned-up man. Virgo might consider loosening up if he enjoys the sexual fringe benefits from his Aquarius woman.

Aquarius is quite the freaky one when it comes to sex. With her, sex is a rollercoaster of many quirky things. She has no qualms displaying her sexual talents, and as long as Virgo holds his sharp tongue, she will keep serving it up to him. She will bring out his passionate side in and out of the bedroom. While Virgo may plan it out, whatever he plans he will deliver, and Aquarius will be pleasured. But, unfortunately, over time the Aquarius woman will get bored. Boredom spells death for this relationship.

Virgo Man/Pisces Woman

Sexually, this can be a perfect match. Their sexual attraction is instant, and each is quite curious about the other. In the bedroom, neither of them needs to be in charge.

In many ways, these two complement each other perfectly. Pisces moves on feeling; Virgo moves on thinking. Pisces wants Prince Charming, and Virgo is a stable, dependable sort who makes her feel safe. Virgo feels secure enough with his Pisces woman to let go, and Pisces finds comfort when she gives her heart to a Virgo.

Sex will be one of the main reasons these two have a lasting relationship. Pisces is adventurous in the bedroom, and Virgo finds this attractive. When Pisces finishes servicing her Virgo man, he will long for more.

But even with all this sexual compatibility, these two sensitive people might find themselves running away as easily as they came together. Pisces will quickly swim away from Virgo if she feels he is trying to manipulate her in any way. Commitment is what is needed if these two are striving for a long-term relationship.

Famous Virgo Men

AUGUST 23–SEPTEMBER 22

Chris Tucker—August 31, 1972
Ludacris—September 11, 1977
Michael Jackson—August 29, 1958
Kobe Bryant—August 23, 1978
Damon Wayans—September 4, 1960
Kel Mitchell—August 25, 1978
Blair Underwood—August 25, 1964
James Lesure—September 21, 1975
Alfonso Ribero—September 21, 1971

Libra

September 23–October 22

Your Libra Man

On first inspection, Libra is the perfect mate: intelligent, classy, affectionate, helpful and kind. He has high morals and will fight to the death for what he believes is right. He is a huge champion of the underdog, which is why many Libras go into the field of Criminal Justice.

His sign is represented by the scales, so Libra has a need to find balance and harmony in everything he does. Your Libra man doesn't have any problem showing you his masculine side while also sharing his emotional, feminine side. He can't help himself. He just likes to keep things in perfect symmetry.

Libra is not the one to jump into things, especially relationships. Sure, he's adventurous enough to give most things a try, but when it comes to love, he's a slowpoke. He is the type of man who can date a woman for years before deciding that it's actually a relationship. It's not that he doesn't want to marry; in fact, as a total romantic, he craves that happily ever after. But he'll weigh the pros and cons of a relationship to see how things are working, how they're balancing out, before he makes any permanent decisions. I know a Libra who dated a sister for seventeen years before proposing marriage.

Closely linked to this slow and steady approach to relationships is the Libra's tendency to procrastinate. He's not exactly a take-charge guy, and you might be shocked when you notice that he actually gets things done. He's unsure about his choices and worries about the ramifications, so he's often frozen with fear about making a mistake. Choices are so difficult for the Libra male that if you go out to a restaurant, it's best to choose a place with the shortest menu possible. Otherwise, he'll take forever to decide on an order and then he'll rattle off a list of requests straight out of the Meg Ryan scene in the movie *When Harry met Sally*.

While he might take a long time to make a choice and settle down with one woman, the Libra has no shortage of women to choose from. Women love the Libra male and flock around him like butterflies, vying for his attention. He is so easygoing and good-humored that he always makes a woman feel smart or sexy or interesting. The Libra has a sort of sixth sense. He can spot a woman's insecurities and always knows how to make her feel better about herself. He is a true chameleon, changing from one thing to the next in order to please a woman. His deep understanding of women and his ability to form a kinship with sisters make them trust him easily.

If you're looking for the faithful type, there is a good chance you'll be disappointed by the Libra. He needs to be surrounded by beauty, and he always seems to be looking for the next thing to catch his interest. Life is too short for just one woman. And even if you get him to be sexually monogamous, he's not going to stop talking to the harem of women in his life, because they all mean something to him. He won't keep his other women a secret, and he won't push a woman toward a relationship because he doesn't want to be responsible for breaking a sister's heart. While most men who juggle women like the Libra are called dogs, this sign is so aware of flaws, including his inability to go deep, that you empathize with him.

Libra likes the type of woman who is willing to take over his care and feeding. While he is capable of fending for himself, he'd prefer it if she did the job for him. This includes footing the bill for the shopping sprees he loves but isn't always able to afford. Libra can be a spendthrift, which means his finances aren't necessarily in the best condition. If you get with a Libra man, be prepared; your checkbook might get quite a workout. Libra will typically marry up—and I'm sure you can guess why. He certainly isn't interested in marrying anyone with less than he came from.

The reason Libra loves to shop is because he is constantly on the lookout for beautiful things. He takes great pride in his appearance and must always be camera-ready. Unlike a Gemini, Sagittarius or Leo, this isn't the brother who wants people stopping by unannounced. This is exactly the type of thing that can throw this brother off balance, and that's never a good thing for a Libra. So if you're the type to holler out "Honey, the girls are coming over to hang," you would be wise to have a Plan B lined up. Libra believes in doing things the right way, and that means time to prepare both himself and his household.

While the Libra is busy making rules for you about your friends—when they come over, how long they can stay, etc.—don't expect to have any say about his friendships, and even less input when it come to his family. He depends on his support team to balance out his life. If you try to pick and choose his friends, this calm, sensible Libra will turn on you. He needs these people in order to feel secure, and removing any of his friends is like taking a security blanket from a baby. It's not worth the fight.

Speaking of fighting, it's never a good idea to make a Libra jealous. When you upset him, he can rage for hours, and who wants that? And when a Libra fights, it's not always fair. He's not above manipulation to keep you in line. He'll expect you to always put him first, but don't expect the same in return. Even if you are a "keeper" and he makes you his woman, you will always be reminded that you better continue to live up to his standards, or he'll move on to the next woman. And don't think he won't do it, either.

If you're not handling business and holding it down, the Libra usually has someone on the side willing to make him feel valuable and desirable. This won't always include sex. He'll get caught up with another woman because he needs attention and romance the same way most people need food and water, and if you force him to do without it, he'll get it somewhere else.

At the same time, Libra has an almost desperate need to merge with another person in a relationship, so if you're keeping him happy, chances are he'll want to marry you. Librans love to get married and live out their fantasies of domesticated bliss. If you're the type of woman who loves to take care of her man, and you're confident enough to handle all the other exes and female friends he refuses to cut loose, then you might just be able to find happily ever after with a Libra man.

Let's Get It Started

The Libra man is always on a search for balance and harmony. He likes to have a good time, but he wants to know that there is no price to pay in the end, no consequences that will upset his balance. This is why he likes a trusting woman who won't freak out every time he glances in the direction of another woman. In fact, you could point out a few of the hottest women in the club for him to admire, and this will really get him going. Libra likes women who are a bit on the wild side. He wants a lady in the bedroom, but he needs to know you're not too uptight, and that you can let go and hang.

He wants to bed the star of the movie and not her stand-in, so if you want this man, then bring your confidence. Let him see you surrounded by a group of adoring males. He'll sit on the sidelines with a devilish smile on his lips as he watches you work your bad girl magic. Libra wants the woman everybody has to have. In other words, if nobody in the room is checking for you, neither is Libra. Don't even bother to approach this brother if you're not wearing your hottest outfit and your hair and makeup aren't perfect.

Once you've had your fun flirting with each other at the club, make a date for dinner at your place, which must be something out of *Architectural Digest*. The Libra loves beautiful things. He likes the stage set for seduction, whether or not there is going to be a happy ending, so go ahead and entertain his senses. Light some scented candles and offer him a glass of expensive wine. He'll want a luxurious meal, but he won't care if you're domestic at all, so go ahead and order takeout. As far as the Libra is concerned, that's why they have restaurants in the first place. As long as you're paying the bill and the food is gourmet, he'll be impressed.

Dinner conversation will flow easily as long as you remember this simple rule: Admire, admire, admire. Libra views himself as a work of art, so it's best you two get on the same page. People always accuse the Leo of having a huge ego, but the Libra's ego is just as big—not that he'd ever let you know it. When giving him a compliment, think outside the box and make it memorable. He gets compliments from plenty of women, so you need to be sure yours is the one he remembers. Admire his designer outfit, but take it a step further and tell him you think it was a wise investment for him to buy high quality clothes. He'll appreciate you for stroking his ego, and won't even notice if you're lying.

Just keep in mind that if a relationship develops, he will expect you to continue heaping praise on him. This is a man who is not afraid to have a little something on the side, so it's a good idea to pay close attention to him. He's a visual creature, so you must look appealing to him at all times. If you snag a Libra and you want to keep him happy, be ready to work hard.

Keeping Him Happy

- Wear the latest fashion.
- Give him lots of freedom.
- Don't ever complain about his need to spend money on luxury.
- Take some self improvement classes with him.
- Keep the compliments coming.
- Throw him a surprise birthday party.
- Stay in shape.

Sex

Just because so many gigolos are born under this sign doesn't mean you should avoid the Libra male. He's so easygoing and low key that he doesn't trip on anything sexual. Lots of fun can be had with a Libra male in the bedroom. He won't pressure you for sex, but there is something so sexual about him that before you know it, you're begging him for some.

The straight Libra male is often accused of being bisexual, but it's only because he doesn't care to play the macho role. His sign is a balance between the two sexes, which means he isn't afraid to show his soft side. And there are some benefits to a man who is in touch with his feminine side. This brother can sense just what will please his woman. In the bedroom, he wants to be sure you have a satisfying experience. He can turn up the testosterone in bed if that's what he senses you want, morphing into a horny, masculine animal as he ravages your body.

Hopefully you're the kind of sister who doesn't mind the whole friends with benefits thing, because with a Libra, that is often all he is offering. But he won't play games with you, either. He doesn't like hurting anyone, so he'll be honest about where you two stand. He just wants to chill with you, so don't expect the sex to be anything more than casual—no strings attached.

Libra often takes a vow of sexual abstinence, waiting until the mood hits him—which could take a while. When he's not in the mood for sex, dancing around in a G string won't do anything to excite him. He is famously a mind over matter type of guy, so he won't be swayed until he is ready. The trick with the Libra is to let go and have a good time without worrying about the pace.

When the mood does hit him, the best way to please him is to make it clear how much you appreciate him. Just like outside the bedroom, Libra loves to receive praise. He'll wants to hear you moan and groan and call out his name. Compliment him on the size of his package and how good it makes you feel when he's inside of you. Comment on how good he smells, how good he tastes. The vain Libra has probably gone to great lengths to prepare for your sexual encounter, and it will excite him to know that you've noticed.

When it's his turn to take care of you, Libra likes to kiss the inside of your thighs, teasing you as he licks closer to your honey pot, but he won't be rushed, no matter how many times you beg to be eaten. He's not trying to torture you; he just likes to take his time building to an orgasm. If you want it to move quicker than the Libra's pace, then you have to take control and slide on top. Just be sure you do it in a feminine manner, since the Libra will lose his erection if he's pushed too hard. Just be patient, because you'll be happy you waited.

Libra Turn-Ons

- Slow dancing.
- A woman's curves.
- Role playing and costumes, especially where he is the one in control.
- Watching you masturbate for his entertainment.
- Casual encounters.
- Incense and candles.
- Threesomes where he is the center of attention.
- High heels on a naked woman.
- Loud moans and calling his name during sex.
- Watching you perform a private striptease for him.
- Mirrored ceilings.

Moving On Without Drama

Libra can't stand to hurt anyone, so this is one where you'll definitely have to do all the work if you're ready to end the relationship. Your goal must be to give him no choice but to walk away—into the waiting arms of one of the other women in his harem, of course.

Remember that the Libra is all about balance in his life, so as a starting point, find ways to throw things off kilter. Change up everything that he's come to expect from you as far as behavior, appearance, and temperament. He won't know what hit him.

If you're in a relationship with a Libra, then no doubt you've been heaping him with so much praise that he's come to expect it on an hourly basis. Stop complimenting him on his appearance, and act unimpressed in the bedroom. When he wears a new outfit for the first time, instead of telling him how sexy looks in it, ask him how much it cost. Then, no matter what price he tells you, tell him he paid too much and you think he ought to start saving some money.

Money is a sensitive issue for a Libra, and he'll lose interest in you quickly if he thinks your generosity is drying up. Let him know that you'll be tightening your purse strings, so you expect him to start clipping coupons and buying generic. The next time you take him out to dinner, make it a cheap, tacky theme restaurant. Libra doesn't think of himself as a mere mortal; he wants special treatment all the time and can't stand to wait in lines, so the long wait at this type of restaurant will drive him crazy.

Stop making him feel pampered at home too. Treat the house like a hotel, and get annoyed if he asks you to clean up. Tell your friends to stop by anytime they feel like it, so your Libra man will be caught unprepared for their visits. This works even better if you extend the invitation to your rowdiest friends, who will come over and disturb the peaceful home that the Libra requires. In fact, why not ask them to bring their kids and stay for a long weekend?

While you're having a great time with your friends, drop plenty of hints about how much you disapprove of his friends and family. Do the same with his choice in fashion and his hairstyle. Call him shallow. Basically, become completely

negative about everything he likes, and everything you once told him you loved about him.
Libra has a hard enough time being faithful, so
before long, he'll have a new lover and a sugar
momma on the side, and he won't even notice
that you're gone.

Compatibility

LIBRA

Libra Man/Aries Woman

Since opposites attract, these two can attract their way into a deep, dark sexual life. Outside of the bedroom, however, they are usually off in different directions, and if it weren't for the sex, they might pass each other right by.

Aries will be taken by Libra's charm and his easygoing nature. One area where he won't be so easygoing, though, is her wardrobe. Aries likes her outfit to reflect her mood, but Libra will break out in hives if he's near the color purple. Aries might have to let her Libra man have control over her choice of clothing.

They both love to be loved and each wants the other one to give a stamp of approval, but Libra needs more pampering. Unfortunately, Aries's schedule rarely permits her to hang around long enough to take care of her man like that. Libra understands the give and take of sex, while Aries has a hard time with compromise. If they could stay naked and tangled up between the sheets, sex might keep them together. Unfortunately, Aries has places to go.

Libra Man/Taurus Woman

These two are ruled by the planet of love and beauty. Libra's lovemaking is romantic and in good taste, but this lusty Taurus woman can unleash him for a good old romp in the sack. Oral sex is a winner with these two, and a way to loosen things up if needed. Sounds good so far, right? Not so fast.

Libra will have to try not to unleash every issue floating through his mind, trying to sway her to his way of thinking. They would also benefit if Taurus put her bullish side away and met him halfway. Slipping into bed with a sweet dish of something to eat might help shut their mouths and arouse their sexual senses to get them in the right mood for some serious hot sex.

Both of these signs love to shop, which is a huge problem because no one is watching the bank account. Libra likes to be on the go, while Taurus is a homebody and likes him to be in her boudoir doing what she expects him to do. Unless these two learn to compromise, they don't have a chance of making it as a couple.

Libra Man/Gemini Woman

Sex with them is exciting. They are both air signs, open to try anything. Gemini's sex is wild, and Libra will jump right in and add a few of his own moves.

Attraction with this duo begins with the mind. They can talk and talk and talk. They also love a good flirt—with others, that is. But when Gemini whips some of her sexy games on him, Libra is ready to pay attention to her.

Libra knows not to crowd Gemini; she needs her space. And she is too busy to notice that he's always on the go too. But when they're together, they can stay in bed and keep each other going for hours. Neither the Gemini nor the Libra requires a partner to get too emotionally attached. It bores the Gemini and it unbalances the Libra. If he doesn't exhaust himself trying to keep up, they might find their union will have a lasting chance.

Libra Man/Cancer Woman

The Cancer woman could feel safe with her Libra man, if only he were better able to make a decision. His long-winded nature can leave Cancer feeling insecure.

The sex will be enjoyable, and often romance will spark. Cancer will enjoy when her Libra man has an orgasm just as much as her own climax. Her lovemaking is often laced with her sensitivity, and she might find herself crying at the peak of her orgasm, whereas Libra will retreat. Although Cancer is the sexy zodiac sign, she keeps her sex simple. Adventure is not high on her list, unless her partner initiates it. Libra likes to get dirty between the sheets.

Cancer wants to be connected to her partner from the soul. This may not be on Libra's to-do list. He likes to keep things light, and too much neediness makes him uncomfortable. He likes his women to be independent of him, but Cancer wants her man to need her as much as she needs him. The only hope for a long-term union between these two is if they never had to leave the bedroom.

Libra Man/Leo Woman

This love match is exciting and romantic. Libra is turned on by Leo's overt sexuality. If he were so inclined, he could easily enjoy sex with her inside a public restroom. Libra doesn't mind if Leo takes the lead, as long as he gets his chance to add some freak to the mix. Leo shouldn't let Libra's nice guy demeanor fool her. He can get downright freaky and have her swapping and even watching him with a transsexual. As long as his focus is on her, she won't mind most of what Libra suggests.

They have such a great time together in bed, separating can be difficult. If they can keep from hurting each other's feelings, they might find they can stay together for a lasting relationship.

Libra Man/Virgo Woman

Good sex, trust issues. That is where Virgo stands in this union. Libra loves to show his romantic side to his Virgo woman. She will feel like a queen because he will put her on top of his pedestal—that is until she starts criticizing him about the height.

Sex will be easy and smooth. They will each take care of the other's sexual needs, but Virgo won't be nearly as sexual as Libra likes. Libra does not care to be tied down, unless it's in the bed with his Virgo on top of him. He's unpredictable and likes it like that. Virgo will find that she doesn't trust his commitment, and that will make it hard for her to get busy in the bedroom.

Although it's not likely these two can go the distance, they just might make it work. Look at Virgo woman, Jada Pinkett Smith and Libra, Will Smith.

Libra Man/Libra Woman

Sexually, these two are willing to have fun and have it often. A romantic setting will get both of them in the mood. Candles, music, rose petals, incense, aromatherapy: Libras like to dress it up. Put them in a room, and after a few hours, it will be filled with steam.

A Libra couple will also carry that heat with them outside of the bedroom. They are the couple that friends admire. They surround themselves with beauty and continuously work to keep things in synch. The Libra/Libra combo spends much of their time shopping and working to make themselves and their environment perfect. They are both so busy trying to find balance and harmony that if they're out of synch, it's painful. If you want to know true meaning of oneness, take a look at two Libras in love.

Libra Man/Scorpio Woman

These two could have a good weekend fling, but not much more. Unless you're into emotional rollercoasters, this is a combination to be avoided.

Let's start with jealousy. Libra's need for attention and his roaming eye will result in constant suspicions from Scorpio. He will have to jump through hoops to convince Scorpio he's not sleeping around. She will require proof: things like the check that shows he only paid for one dinner, and allowing her to glance at the incoming and outgoing calls on his cell phone. Libra won't be able to handle Scorpio's drama, and he'll go missing when she becomes possessive.

The discussions (or arguments, depending on who's telling the story) will end up driving Libra into the arms of another woman. Once that line is crossed, it's basically a wrap. Scorpio is not the forgiving type. She will continuously remind him of his "bad" behavior, and when that gets old, look out. Her revenge monster will rear its ugly head.

If these two want this relationship to be more than just a fling, she will have to learn to relax and he will have to keep his roaming eye on one person. If only it were that easy.

Libra Man/Sagittarius Woman

There is no need to know how things are going to work out for these two; they just love the idea of being in love. Libra and Sagittarius are two romantic individuals. Libra will go for the candles, wine and roses, and a nice romantic setting. Sag can cut through all that floss and get to the meat. His meat.

These two are quite the sexual pair. Pleasing Sagittarius in the bedroom is one of the highlights for Libra. She is always ready to try out some of her wild positions with him.

Besides the bedroom, there are other areas where this pair works well. Sag is a big dreamer, and Libra loves to help her bring them to fruition. Ms. Sagittarius loves Mr. Libra's laid back approach to life, and Libra knows how to appeal to her intellect. She loves to plays dress up for him, and he just loves beautiful things. These are two outgoing people who love socializing with popular people. Both like to spend money on extravagances, and they somehow manage to keep it coming.

In Sagittarius, the Libra has found a partner who will allow him to be himself without judgment or resentment. These are two signs of the zodiac that have a good chance for a happy relationship.

Libra Man/Capricorn Woman

Capricorn is ready to teach her Libra man quite a few sexual tricks! At first, the sexual and romantic compatibility will be subtle, but over time, it will get hotter. Capricorn finds a Libra man enticing, and Libra is drawn to Capricorn's strong sexuality.

On the other hand, they might have some problems outside of the bedroom. Libra is known to be quite sentimental and is in love with love, while Capricorn, who is realistic, won't have much tolerance for this. Capricorn wants to know that what Libra says is absolute and true. She's not interested in this constant changing of the mind. Libra will make her his number one, but unfortunately for him, her ambitions will always come before him.

Cap is a loner. She can get by on the company of one or two friends, while Libra prefers the nightlife and an audience, especially of the opposite sex. When it's time for Libra to slow down, he wants to relax and contemplate his life. Capricorn, on the other hand, prefers to always be working on something. If these two were able to straighten out some of their crucial differences, they might have a go at it for a while. But in general, this romance is short-lived.

Libra Man/Aquarius Woman

Together, this pair can discuss anything. When they meet, there is an immediate emotional connection that will leave them feeling they have just met their perfect, lifelong mate.

Those feelings are confirmed again when they are engrossed in a passionate night of lovemaking.

The best thing about this pair is their free approach to sex. They thrive on mental and sexual energy. And since they are both attracted to freaky sex, each night will be a new adventure for them. They put all their sexual, emotional energy to good use. Sex is so off the charts because neither of them has any rules.

When those bedroom doors fly open and they step out of fantasy, a beautiful and calming environment works well to create balance and harmony for this pair. They will find their friendship to be an enjoyable one. Aquarius appreciates how

Libra loves to focus his attention on her and how he bends over backwards to please her. She takes it all in.

Beautiful friendship, wonderful socializing skills, and shared cultural interests, this is the perfect dating match for the Aquarius woman and the Libra man. However, their business skills and money issues might be the downfall of all this love and harmony.

Libra Man/Pisces Woman

This duo will have good sex, but don't expect a long-term anything. Libra and Pisces might have some challenges to deal with early on in their relationship.

Pisces will find she has found the classy man of her dreams and want to show him off to the world. Libra has found stability and security in his Pisces woman. A romantic evening is inevitable. Slow dancing and a tall glass of something bubbly will be the prelude for the sexy music these two will make as the night goes on. A warm bubble bath, a hot oil massage and caressing each other's bodies will follow. Sex will be beautiful, with a steady rhythm, and passionate, very passionate pushing.

After such an evening, Pisces whose emotions have gotten caught up, might feel it's time to make this a legal affair. But Libra is a major procrastinator and would never make a lifelong decision without careful thought. If Pisces can be patient, these two might have something. As long as they stay true to each other and avoid secrets, even those little secrets, a Libra man and a Pisces woman should be headed for a wonderful, lasting union.

Famous Libra Men

SEPTEMBER 23–OCTOBER 22

Nick Cannon—October 8, 1980
Russell Simmons—October. 4, 1957
Snoop Dogg—October. 20, 1971
Will Smith—September 25, 1968
Bernie Mac—October 5, 1957
Demond Wilson—October 13 1946
Omar Gooding—October. 19, 1976
Usher—October 14, 1978
Jermaine Dupri—September 23, 1972
Wyclef Jean—October 17, 1972

Scorpio

October 23–November 21

Your Scorpio Man

Much has been written about the manipulative and possessive Scorpio man, but believe me when I tell you that this water sign has gotten a bad rap. It's not that those negative traits don't exist; it's that the positive characteristics are never discussed.

Scorpio is the most loyal friend or lover you will ever find. He's extremely giving of himself and can't say no if a friend or family member needs his time or advice. If you're on the road to success and need some pointers, he will never turn you away. As long as you have dreams that you believe in and the passion behind them, this is a man who will support and champion your ideas.

Another Scorpio trait that most people tend to forget about is his tremendous capacity for compassion. Yeah, he's got a bleeding heart, and loves to be of service in the world, helping others.

Scorpio loves his family and considers his closest friends part of his family. Think of the Scorpio man as the Marlon Brando character in *The Godfather*. Anybody Scorpio loves is under his protection and should never be tampered with. If you are lucky enough to be included in this list, you'll feel comfortable going out on a ledge because if you fall for any reason, the Scorpio has your back.

He's got a strong shoulder and will let you cry on it, but if he thinks you are becoming dependent in an unhealthy way, he'll shove you up on your two feet and out the door. He is far from a doormat and will expect all those in his life to be independent. To earn loyalty and respect from a Scorpio, you must be a pretty special woman.

Some signs like a passive rag doll for a mate, but the Scorpio needs a spiritual, intellectual and sexual equal. This brother is too suspicious to welcome the overeager types who seem to be in awe of him. He needs a woman with confidence in her own abilities. He likes smart, interesting, and independent people. He is a natural born leader, but he's not seeking out followers. He prefers people who forge their own paths.

Once the Scorpio male sets his sights on a female, all bets are off. If he wants her and believes they share a soul connection, her unavailability won't stop him from pursuing a relationship. Even if a woman is in a marriage or committed relationship when she catches the Scorpio's eye, he'll go after her in such an intense manner that she'll feel like the most desirable woman in the world.

To the Scorpio man, no one is off-limits. He possesses enough charm and magnetism to melt his toughest critic. I know a Sagittarius female who considered a certain Scorpio male "a joke" and didn't find one redeemable quality about him. She hated his smile, his laugh, his hype and everything in between.

He arranged for a mutual friend to bring her to a function he was throwing. Before long, he had cast his spell on the Sagittarius, who kept saying, "I don't know how this happened because he's not my type." All the while, she couldn't stop thinking about him.

He is a lethal combination of sexiness, confidence and experience. Perfect examples of a Scorpio men are Sean Combs and Nelly. Both these men are hardworking, multitalented, have music careers, fashion lines and tend to date independent, successful women.

This is a man who knows exactly what he is working with.

His over-inflated ego didn't get that way by accident. And when every woman he's ever slept with brags about his prowess, he's bound to feel good about his skills. He'll also make. sure he lives up to his insatiable reputation.

Until a Scorpio is ready to settle down, he will keep it moving, sliding from one woman to another as if he's trying to squeeze the most out of life in a short amount of time. He is an expert at juggling many women, all the while making each one feel special and important to him. But it's not that he's lying. He genuinely can find something valuable about each and every woman that he meets. He has the unique gift of honing in and figuring out exactly who a woman is and what she needs, even if she hasn't figured that out yet. So don't get too close unless you're willing to fall all the way in.

And if you do fall for a Scorpio, be prepared to deal with some intensely emotional moments. The Scorpio male is incapable of hiding whatever he is thinking. Every thought that crosses his mind shows up on his face like a computer screen. If he's unhappy with you, there is no way you'd ever be confused, especially after he gives you his dismissive glare.

He does tend to let emotions get the best of him, especially when he feels betrayed. And watch out! When he gets mad, furniture gets broken, cars get crashed and feelings get hurt. So when you see a Scorpio storm brewing, it's best to run and hide—immediately!

If you are a woman who likes an extremely passionate man and you're hoping to one day lure a Scorpio man to your side of the street, you need confidence, nerves of steel and the ability to never let him see you sweat. This man is turned on by his own power, so you better have some of your own. If you disappoint him, he will get rid of you immediately. I never said it was easy to love a Scorpio man, but what I can promise is that it will never be boring.

Let's Get It Started

This man loves nothing more than to hear how great you think he is. Two people completely focused on him is the Scorpio male idea of heaven. But if you do compliment him, make sure it's not a lie, because he will see right through you. You have to be real to get anywhere with this man. If you try to fool him with lies, he'll know it and hold it against you. He doesn't like any form of deception.

One way to show him you're sincerely interested is to look him straight in the eyes while you give him compliments. He likes when people are paying attention and will notice if you shift it away from him even a little bit. Don't let his intensity intimidate you; instead, hold his gaze for as long as you can and you'll win his respect. Scorpio needs to respect a woman, even if he's only planning to bring her home for a one-night stand.

Scorpio wants to be impressed with the woman in his life. That doesn't mean she can't go through a rough patch, but it means he won't put up with someone trying to ride his coat tails. You need to have your own dreams, your own friends and your own life in order to attract the attention of a Scorpio male.

He learned a long time ago that life is not fair and well, if he can deal with that inconvenient truth, then you should be able to. Show him that you have a hard enough shell to deal with life's trials and tribulations. Tell him about the way you stood up to your boss at work or how you demanded to be treated fairly by your siblings in childhood. He likes a woman with some spunk, and if she can make him laugh, she's halfway to his heart.

Talk about interesting subjects. This is a guy who you can get into some heated discussions about sex, religion, politics or anything else. He is turned on by intelligence, so bone up on your current events and know what's going on in the world. Let him in on your vast accomplishments.

Showing him your intelligence can be a delicate balancing act, though. It's important to have your own interests, but let him know that if you were his woman, he'd come first. When it comes to attraction, his goal is to have better sex today than he had yesterday—and by the way, the sex yesterday was fantastic. He needs to know immediately that you're a giving person and that you don't expect the relationship to be all about you. So mention some recent good deed you performed.

Just be sure that the good deed wasn't helping an ex-boyfriend. Scorpio is extremely jealous and he doesn't ever want to be reminded that his woman had lovers before him. To avoid an uncomfortable situation, don't take him anyplace where you might run into other men you've slept with. This will not impress him; it'll turn him off completely.

The same goes for men you might want to bed in the future. Scorpio will dismiss you in an instant if he sees you flirting with any other men in the place. Focus all your attention on him, and he might just take you up on that offer to come home with you.

If you tell him you'll make him breakfast, just be prepared for a long night ahead. And if you show him the right combination of intelligence, confidence and discretion, then you might just have a chance of making it past a one-night stand.

Keeping Him Happy

- Avoid crass behavior.
- Be confident and independent.
- Tell him he's great in bed.
- Take him to beautiful places—where there is a bed.
- Wear tight, sexy clothes.
- Bring him expensive champagne.
- Take care of him.
- Give up all the other men, even if he keeps a harem.
- Keep a photo of him on your nightstand.
- Be sensitive.

Sex

The Scorpio man was born to have sex, and he's well aware of it. He has sex on the brain 24/7, and can come on like a horny animal just released from a cage. To him, half the fun of having sex is a combination of pain/pleasure. If you're looking for a calm sexual ride, then slide past this brother because he's the scary roller-coaster in the amusement park. He wants to make sure you're having a thrilling time.

He wants to feel good and bad at the same time, so he'll assume you want the same thing. Scorpio will twist your nipples and pinch your vagina, which is a clue for you to tug at his nipples and pinch his penis. He'll holler out in pain, but you'll notice that devilish smile on his face. He'll come on strong from the beginning, smashing his lips into yours in a rough and ready way. This isn't for the faint of heart; this is for grownups only. He gets pleasure from watching his partner in pain during sex.

He's the best pussy eater you've ever met and he knows it. Brotherman will stay down there until you're coming out of your mind and begging for mercy. After he's made you weak from coming, he'll take total control and ravage you. You'll notice that his penis gets harder the more control he has over you.

The Scorpio man likes his women to be submissive. He believes that a woman wants to be dominated, and if you don't stop him, he'll have you starring in his rape fantasies where he takes you against your will. He expects his fantasies to turn you on and will expect you to writhe and scream out in pleasure and pain. If you're not feeling it, then give him a chance to try to do it differently.

Don't be surprised at his collection of sex toys and his interest in porn. You'll find porn magazines dating back to high school. He has a problem giving up any of his sexual tools, even if they're outdated.

Scorpio is fascinated by the dark side of sex: S&M, swinging, cross dressing, porn, bondage, and prostitution. He'll insist on going to a swingers' party, but don't expect him to join in. It'll depend on how he feels at that moment. Remember this brother is a water sign, so you must follow the Scorpio's ever-changing moods.

As much as Scorpio likes and needs sex, if he loves you and you don't satisfy him, he'll get his needs met elsewhere and not consider it cheating. Because he's such a freak, he doesn't understand a woman who can't loosen up in bed. In fact, if you need to get up early for work, plan on drinking lots of coffee because this is a man who can have sex all day, every day.

If you're looking for a man who will never let your sex life die no matter how long you're together, then the Scorpio brother is the one to stick with. He'll keep you screaming out for more, and to him, that's doing a great job. Scorpio is the sign that governs the sex organs, so he'll need to know that he's satisfied you. He will work to open you up and to help you see things his way and before long, you'll be completely sprung.

Scorpio Turn-Ons

- Hot, steamy sex all night long.
- Women who are not shy in the bedroom.
- Spanking, pinching, biting and other forms of S&M.
- Cunnilingus.
- Sex toys, especially handcuffs he can use on you.
- Porno magazines, videos, websites.
- Group sex.
- Making a woman come until she screams.

Moving On Without Drama

If you've met the love of your life (and it isn't him) and you want to end your thing with Scorpio, please do us all a favor and keep that information to yourself. He isn't the type to wish you well. It's much more likely he'll put you in a hospital. He does not take the removal of his sexual partner lightly.

With most signs, you can slink away with your tail between your legs, lying about the reasons why you aren't good enough for them. But the Scorpio will see right through that speech and punish you for trying to con him. He'll threaten to ruin you, your reputation and any relationship you're thinking of starting. When he's been hurt, he'll hit way below the belt and make sure he has an audience to watch you fall. You won't believe that the charming fellow who made you feel like the most amazing woman in the world is now out to destroy you.

You might not want to end it straight up, unless you'd like to get more than your heart broken. In order to save your car, your ego, your reputation and your head in a breakup, use your brains. Manipulate him into being the one who chooses to leave, but don't ever let him know that he's being played.

Use each and every one of the tactics on the list below, and don't let up even for a second. If you keep him busy enough with these behaviors, you'll get him to leave without too much drama.

- Brag about more successful men in your life.
- Tell him you're too tired for sex, no matter how tempted you are by his powers of seduction.
- Accuse him of being too dominating.
- Stop participating in any of your usual hobbies or interests.
- Become clingy and needy.
- Accuse him of cheating. Question every move he makes.
- Complain about how powerless you feel at work.
- Run out of interesting things to talk about, so there are plenty of awkward silences between you.

If you follow these directions, it won't take long before he's moved on and you can breathe a big sigh of relief.

Compatibility

SCORPIO

Scorpio Man/Aries Woman

These two possess lots of power. They are strong individuals. A relationship that could be headed for hot sex and fun can also turn out to be a disaster if these two are not careful.

Both like to be the center of their universe and they expect to come first. Scorpio is too controlling for Aries. And the Aries woman is a challenge for the Scorpio man as well, because she won't be tied down or let anyone tell her what to do. She has courage, and does not easily back down.

In the bedroom, these two can release their sexual tension and it will set off fireworks. They are not afraid to try anything new sexually. Scorpio might be pleasantly surprised if Aries whips out the handcuffs, but Aries should expect that he will chain her to the bed with those handcuffs.

No matter who's on top, sex will be hot, though it will unfortunately be short-lived.

Scorpio Man/Taurus Woman

There will be lots of intense lovemaking, whenever, wherever, and for whatever reason. These two complete each other. Their relationship goes deep; mind, body and soul.

Scorpio has a way of summoning his woman, any woman, without speaking a word. If Taurus passes a sexy man at a party and feels an overwhelming sensation to connect with him, he's probably a Scorpio.

Scorpio craves a loyal, loving partner, who makes him feel like the most important person in her life. Taurus fits this bill well. She likes to take care of her man and loves to play dress up for her Scorpio, who always appreciates her effort.

Their sexual union will have such intensity, they will feel like newly transformed people. Even though this duo can be possessive of each other, there is the possibility of a long-lasting relationship.

Scorpio Man/Gemini Woman

A Scorpio man's sexual experience will take a Gemini woman to new heights. Sexual games will definitely be on the menu for Scorpio and Gemini. These two will have lots of sex, so who cares if she's distracted once the two of them close those bedroom doors? Well, Scorpio might.

Outside of the bedroom, he might find it's hard to keep her interested. She can be fickle, distracted, and curious. She can be a chatter-box, wanting to discuss every issue going on in the world. Scorpio can only talk about politics or global warming once in a while, but Gemini can go on for days. Scorpio wants to control the Gemini, and the Gemini wants to be free.

Amazing sex is part of Gemini and Scorpio's zodiac connection, but with all their differences, it's amazing these two ever make it to the bed-room. Unfortunately, or fortunately, depending on how you view it, there is no way these two can have a satisfying relationship away from the bedroom.

Scorpio Man/Cancer Woman

A delightful experience indeed. The sexual connection between a Scorpio man and a Cancer woman goes deep to the soul. They are both domestic and love making their home a place to spend hours upon hours. When they're together, it's about them and no one else.

Cancer feels sexy with her Scorpio mate. After all, they connect so deeply, they have the best sex either has ever experienced. Scorpio feels confident that he is able to uplift his mate and help her to feel her uniqueness. Scorpio loves Cancer's loyalty. Cancer enjoys taking care of him. If they made love in a church, it couldn't be any more spiritually connected.

They have a telepathic kind of relationship. Each can read the other, which works both positively and negatively. These two can definitely go the long haul, but if either of them is not ready for a relationship, their encounter can scar for life.

Scorpio Man/Leo Woman

There is sexual excitement with this duo, but you might question if they are exciting each other or themselves. The Leo might feel that this relationship, both in and out of the bedroom is all about her. And it wouldn't be fair if Scorpio didn't feel it was all about him.

Scorpio is always ready for some good, bold sex. When Leo is not out being adored by her public, they have a sexy time together. They like to play games with bondage, Kama Sutra, ben-wa balls, handcuffs and any other toys they can find.

When everything lines up for these two and all their egotistical ways are put aside, they can be sexually off the charts.

But Scorpio needs more loyalty than the Leo is willing to give, and the Leo needs more attention than she can get from him. Scorpio will turn off quickly if he feels ignored. Once they step out of the bed, they just don't make sense.

They should try putting a bed in every room of the house, and then this just might work. Who cares about a relationship when the sex is this good?

Scorpio Man/Virgo Woman

These two can bring out the best in each other. Earth and water are loyal partners, and sex between them will have meaning.

Virgo will go slower, while Scorpio is ready to try every new position and fantasy ever dreamed of. Once Scorpio helps Virgo to relax and unleash her inner wildness, they will go to new sexual heights. He needs to be patient and understanding with Virgo's slow tendencies. She has to plan out her life, and she doesn't trust when things go too fast. It will frustrate him from time to time, but once they arrive at a harmonious sexual pace, their relationship takes on a deeper meaning.

This can be a simple affair that leaves them panting and sweaty, or the beginning of something long-term. If Virgo can learn to curb her critical tongue, she may even have a faithful Scorpio. This liaison is definitely worth a try.

Scorpio Man/Libra Woman

This is probably the most intense couple out there. There is undeniable sexual attraction with this pair, but the passion and burning desire that propels them into a night of heated sex will not sustain this couple for long. As much as they are alike, they can't see that what they hate in the other is the same thing they hate in themselves. They find themselves struggling to get the other one to relinquish control.

Scorpio and Libra seem to work better with common goals. Unfortunately, as soon as they become passionate about a subject, you better get out the fire extinguisher, because things are about to explode. They should never consider working as business partners. Both are good with money, but in order to run a successful business, they need more compatible partners.

Socially, Libra is a flirt, which makes Scorpio jealous. He takes commitment and love seriously, and wants his partner to do the same. Libra loves the affection Scorpio showers her with, but still desires attention from—well, anyone she can get it from. Scorpio will try to control Libra, who will not be controlled, and Libra will do the same. This only creates a continuous power struggle.

There is too much going on with this pair to make a lasting anything. This rollercoaster ride winds and twists too much to have fun. Oh, well. There's always the merry-go-round.

Scorpio Man/Scorpio Woman

Scorpio is the sign of extremes. The physical chemistry between two Scorpios is off the charts. Passion and hot, steamy sex can be expected. When they make love, their bodies speak. It's as if they can read each other's minds. Each knows exactly what the other wants without a single word being spoken.

In many ways, a Scorpio man and woman are the same person, and there is great comfort in being with someone who knows you so well. The downside is that it can be boring to be with someone who knows you so well. Depending on how much other relationship issues factor into this union, even great sex will not help this duo make it for the long haul.

When either of these Scorpios have been hurt by the other, they're not likely to forgive or forget. When they disagree, they will go head to head, and the same passion and heat that was displayed in the bedroom will have found its way into their everyday lives.

Scorpios are highly jealous and demanding. Now add that to their need to control, and you have constant arguing and fighting. Since giving in and allowing the other to be right is a struggle, they're not likely to stay together past the sex which is inclined to run its course. Take this duo outside of the warm comforts of their bedroom they will not survive. They should definitely say no to marriage.

Scorpio Man/Sagittarius Woman

Be prepared for fireworks because sexually, this is a good match. These two lean toward erotic, passionate sex and the joy of experimenting with new sexual positions. Unfortunately, with all this sexual compatibility and not much else to sustain the relationship, it's bound to fizzle quickly.

Scorpio is power hungry. He will constantly try to get Sagittarius to cross over to his side of the fence, and there will be consequences for his controlling nature. Sagittarians want to be free to explore. She is claustrophobic and doesn't like to feel trapped in a box.

Scorpio would prefer to have her tied up at all times, including in the bed. Sex for Scorpio is a night of sex. It doesn't have to go any deeper than that. For Sagittarius, it's deeper. Besides the pleasure, there should be the promise of a commitment brewing.

Sag is more playful and humorous than Scorpio. She will laugh out loud at Scorpio and the tantrums he throws when he wants his way. He is just way too demanding for Sagittarius. She will soon find herself ready to take flight. The mutual attraction that was once defined by their sexual appetite will be long gone.

Scorpio Man/Capricorn Woman

Call it a sixth sense or something, but these two will know that they are perfect for each other during their initial meeting. This is one deep connection. If either the Scorpio man or the Capricorn woman is looking to settle down, they might feel like they just met their soul mate.

Sexually, they can turn a simple act of love-making into a deeper, richer, soul-searching experience. Scorpio sometimes has to redirect workaholic Capricorn's attention from work to hours of play. This is great for the Capricorn, as it gives her a place to work off the stress from her day. Scorpio will oblige and supply plenty of stress relief. They have a give and take sexual relationship, allowing each other the opportunity to take the lead.

Both Scorpio and Capricorn are serious about their love affair. The water and earth signs balance each other out. The usual insecurity and demanding ways will give way to comfort. Capricorn loves his magnetism and is attracted to that Scorpio power. The Scorpio feels wonderful with her because of her loyal and trustworthy nature.

Together, they share a sense of purpose that will carry them a long way. The Scorpio and Capricorn ship is sailing and it's a clear day. Feel free to hop aboard.

Scorpio Man/Aquarius Woman

Aquarius is the only sign more emotionally unpredictable than the Scorpio. She's a dreamer who juggles ten projects at once and can't be expected to ever show up on time. The Water Bearer is all over the place, jumping from one project to the next, while our Scorpio male expects his woman to put him first. He's a homebody who wants his woman close to him.

Aquarius will rarely come right out and tell Scorpio to lighten up. Instead, she'll just go missing, not caring that a worried Scorpio is pacing the floors wondering if she's had an accident. When Aquarius shows up hours or days later after an argument, he'll be waiting to scream and hit a few more walls.

Sexually, all that emotional energy is put to good use when these two start knocking boots. Plain and simple, it'll be the best sex Aquarius has ever had. And during Aquarius's unexplained absences, Scorpio will spend most of his time waiting to get more sex.

Aquarius needs freedom, but the Scorpio wants a death grip on the person he loves. If Scorpio can get over the need to check up on her every hour on the hour, and if Aquarius can placate him with a little more consistency, they may have a chance of at least a long winter. At the very least, they'll have the kind of sex you can write home about.

Scorpio Man/Pisces Woman

Who knew that there was a sign more intense than the Scorpio? These two get lost in their emotional connection and neediness. Two water signs always fall in deep, particularly if they're not the same sign.

The romantic dreamer Pisces likes the take-charge Scorpio. Being desired by this strong-willed man puts extra confidence in the Pisces. Scorpio's controlling need to track her every move comes across as protective to her. She's such a sensitive soul that she needs to be led away from her emotions, and Scorpio will do that. He can sit and listen to the Pisces dreams for hours then he'll help her formulate a plan to make those dreams come true. Scorpio loves the devotion she brings to the relationship.

In bed, Pisces is game for whatever Scorpio desires, which means everything. Pisces has no fear of getting lost in the darkness of his sexual world. Both are capable of great eroticism, so don't be surprised if they share similar passions for S&M and bondage. Scorpio might get off making Pisces his slave, but then it'll flip and Pisces will take control in bed.

This couple will have to work harder to get out of bed, since that's where they can be their true selves, away from the prying eyes of the world. There is a good chance this union will last. These two are almost incapable of being casual with each other. It's like they have a sixth sense that this opportunity is rare.

Famous Scorpio Men

OCTOBER 23–NOVEMBER 21

Sean "Diddy" Combs—November 4, 1969
Nelly—November 2, 1974
Michael Beach—October 30, 1963
Jaleel White—November. 17, 1976
Terrence "T.C." Carson—November 19, 1969
Omarion—November 12, 1984
Ike Turner—November 5, 1931
Delroy Lindo—November 18, 1952
Savion Glover—November 19, 1973
Sinbad—November 10, 1956

Sagittarius

November 22–December 21

Your Sagittarius Man

If you want an upbeat, outgoing, fun and spontaneous man who knows how to make sure you always have a great time, then the Sagittarius is the man for you. He can cook like your mama, be your best friend, and give you lots of space when you need it. Sagittarius is extremely independent and knows how to do all the traditional male things like change tires and cut his own hair.

The downside to this is that he can make a woman feel useless with his ability to run the perfect household. He can be so independent that his woman might feel like he doesn't need anyone, including her. The trick with this one is convincing him that he really does need you around.

If you like the type of man who will man-handle you and place demands on you, then this is not the one for you. Sagittarius is a free spirit who has an every man for himself attitude. He needs space to explore everyday life, and gives his woman the same. Now, if you are down for whatever and can move at the drop of a hat, then he has no problem taking you along on his many adventures. But please don't be a stick in the mud or try to stop his fun in any way or you'll be uninvited. The Sagittarius has no problem admitting when something isn't working, usually because someone is trying to cramp his style. Then he'll kick you to the curb quick. It's not that he doesn't want the company. In fact, he would prefer not to travel solo through life; it's just that so many women want to control him with their limitations.

The Sagittarius is the positive thinker of the zodiac and doesn't want a partner who will limit him. He is the perpetual "glass half full" sign in the zodiac, who always expects the best out of life. And it's not that he expects things to come easily to him. He's a hard worker who puts lots of effort into whatever he does, so it makes sense that success follows him wherever he goes. This brother is always looking to improve himself, and if you check his iPod, you'll find some recorded self help books he listens to on a regular basis. If there is something he can do to make his dreams come true, he won't hesitate; even if that includes learning to fly or taking a second language.

As far as Sagittarius is concerned, life is short, and he intends to make the most out of the time he's been given. 'What are we doing tomorrow?' is a big question for him because he likes to fill every day with a steady stream of activities, many of them ending way after dark. He is always preparing and planning for his fabulous future, and if you're a part of his life, that fabulousness includes you—as long as you're someone who can go with his flow.

In work or play, the Sagittarius is easygoing, but not easily intimidated. If you think you can boss the Sagittarius around or make him suddenly become passive, then you don't know anything about the Archer. The Sagittarius doesn't care if you are the Queen of England or a rap star; he will not be impressed, nor will he put up with your crap, so please don't give it to him.

He judges everybody based on how they treat him, and it's as simple as that. If you're nice to him and treat him with respect, then he will do the same to you.

I know a successful Sagittarius photographer who worked at a photo lab during his lean years before he made it. One day his boss, who liked to exert his power by making his workers jump through hoops, demanded that the Sag hurry to fill an order. According to the Sagittarius, something about the boss's tone rubbed him the

wrong way. In his own words, he "didn't appreciate be spoken down to." It turned into something
of a standoff, and Sag's peppy stride slowed to
a crawl. Of course, the Sagittarius was fired for
"sauntering," but he never had a moment of
regret. If you want to get the most out of a Sagittarius, then you better use a tone of respect and
dignity.

Sagittarius is one of the most consistent signs
in the zodiac. If you run into a Sag friend years
after he's become successful, you'll be surprised
how cool he's remained. He's never phony or
affected. No matter how successful the Sag becomes, he will tend to have the dirtiest mouth,
using four letter words like they're going out of
style. He is not the type to ever forget where he
came from. So the best way to stay on his good
side is to keep it real—and letting him know
you're adventurous doesn't hurt.

Sagittarius likes to have fun. In fact, he demands it. He has a natural curiosity for all life
has to offer. If you're the kind who needs things
to be serious and in control, you should keep it
moving. Sag is in it for the knowledge and adventure.

Maybe it's because he lives at such an elevated
pace that Sagittarius has a tendency to have high

highs and low lows. When he sinks into a depression, he will act like his life is coming to an end. You'll rush over, hoping to save the Sagittarius from a fatal suicide attempt, only to find him shaking his groove thing to a new Kanye CD. When he stops dancing, he'll inform you that the little problem he was having got resolved. The maddening thing is that Sagittarius will have forgotten that he was ever unhappy in the first place, while you cancelled an important appointment, dropped everything and rushed over with your bag of tricks to make him feel better.

Now, conversely, if you fall into a funk, don't bother calling the Sag, because he'll accuse you of trying to bring him down by being negative. When you're sick, he won't be the one to nurse you back to health. To be fair, he'll stop at the nearest deli and grab you some chicken soup, but don't expect him to sit at your side while you whine about your aches and pains. It's not his fault you weren't watching where you were going and got run over by a truck! He expects you to get over it quickly if you want his respect.

In a relationship, the male Sagittarius is not always faithful. His desire to experience everything life has to offer translates into a longing to experience the incredible variety of women out there. He likes a steady stream of female attention, and because he's so fun and easygoing, women tend to want him, even if he's unavailable.

The Sag is one of the most generous and kindhearted people in the zodiac. If he loans you rent money and then finds out you took it and went shopping, he'll curse you out, but then he'll be over it in the next five minutes. Sagittarius is incapable of holding a grudge. He has his say loudly, and then moves on. In relationships, he tends to have amnesia, forgetting all the horrible things a mate has done. Unlike the Leo, he won't file your faults away to use them against you another time. He expects people to be their best, but when they're not, they're not. He's not about to let it stop his flow. Sagittarius will almost always give you another chance.

Very few men know how to let their hair down and have a good time as easily as the Sagittarius. If you're lucky, his good time will definitely be your good time.

Let's Get It Started

Sagittarius is attracted to a woman with a larger than life personality and perhaps even a larger than life ego. So if you are the wallflower type, keep looking until you find a man born under a different sign. But if you want an adventure, then get your game on and do what you have to, to reel in this fun-loving man. Sagittarius is a brother who goes after what he wants, so once you get him to notice you and pique his interest with your well-toned body and intelligent conversation, he will pursue you aggressively. Get ready to have some fun.

First off, make sure you are working your assets to their best advantage. He likes to think about the possibility of sex when he's meeting a new woman. When it comes to physical attraction, he needs a woman who's been to the gym lately. She has to be proud of her body because that's the instrument she will use to reel him in. If it hurts your feelings, sorry, but the Sagittarius has never been accused of being deep. He needs to like what he sees, and what he likes is a sexy woman who is feminine, but still looks like she could handle rock climbing or sky diving with him and won't worry about breaking a nail. He works hard and plays hard, and doesn't have much respect for couch potatoes.

Sagittarius is a talkative sign, so don't expect to get a word in unless you can speak fast and confidently. And when you do get the chance to talk, make sure you know what you're talking about. If you tell him you're the best at something, you better be telling the truth. Chances are, this explorer will know just as much as you do about the subject, if not more—and because he's competitive, he won't hesitate to call you out on your errors. If you hit upon a subject he doesn't know much about, consider yourself lucky. Sagittarius will be impressed by a sister who can teach him something.

Hopefully you've read some books on positive thinking before beginning a conversation with a Sagittarius. It's not acceptable to bring this brother down. As soon as the subject takes a negative turn, he'll be moving on to the next possible playmate. Sagittarius just wants to have fun, and won't tolerate a companion who can't go with his flow.

There are so many things the Sagittarius would like to try before he dies, so mention something new or different. Offer to show him a part of town he hasn't explored before, or your favorite Ethiopian restaurant, or a hot new photography exhibit. You'll grab his attention because he's always looking for stimulation and adventure.

Of course, if a friend is having a party, you should invite him to that. Sagittarius is social and likes to be around plenty of interesting people. A concert in the park where he can dance with a lot of strangers is appealing to him. He'll wear a funky outfit that shows off his creativity. Even if the clothes embarrass you, be prepared to smile and ignore the stares of more conservatively dressed folks. If you try to contain the Sag's enthusiasm or make him conform, you'll never get to a second date.

He's Mr. Easygoing, so you must show Sagittarius that you're equally laid back. He's always terrified some woman will try to slow him down and end his good time, so go ahead; be playful and get him laughing and acting silly. Sagittarius likes to be entertained. The worst thing you can do is try to tie him down. Let him know that with you, he'll be able to roam through life freely, having adventures and learning everything he can. It's important to have your own life, too, so that you'll be able to amuse him with tales of your day.

If you make it through the first date and he asks you out again, suggest something out of the ordinary, like sky diving, a balloon ride, horseback riding, or something else in the great outdoors. Even a trip to the zoo might be a possibility, because Sagittarius loves animals. Whatever you choose, take things to the edge to let the adventurous Sagittarius know you'll be down for anything.

Take advantage of his fun-loving, spontaneous nature for as long as it lasts. He might not turn out to be marriage material, he might refuse to give up his other women, but however long you're with the Sagittarius, you can be sure it won't be dull.

Keeping Him Happy

- Surprise him with a trip to Vegas because he loves sin.
- Give him lots of space.
- Be easygoing.
- Keep him laughing.
- Dress over the top sexy.
- Make sure he's always having fun.
- Think and act positively.
- Stay loyal and faithful, but don't expect the same.
- Show him you're independent.

Sex

The Sagittarius male is all about the chase. He will pursue you, wearing you down with his enthusiasm until you cannot imagine being with another man. Unfortunately, the pursuit is the most exciting part for him. He's a man in love with the idea of being in love. That often contributes to his need to spread that love to many partners.

The Sagittarius is known for being fickle in his romantic relationships. He loves life too much to settle for any one person, especially when it comes to sex. Think of the Archer as a man-whore who likes to spread the love wherever he goes. He enjoys his freedom, and will be a better lover if he's not feeling pushed into a relationship.

This is the most sexually liberal sign of the zodiac, so he's always down for whatever.

When it comes to the business of two consenting adults, the Archer makes no apologies for going for it. He's into both anal and oral sex, so don't be surprised if he flips from one hole to the next. Sagittarius will try anything at least once. That way, he knows if he likes something.

I know a gay Sagittarius male who had been out of the closet since birth. One day, a woman friend asked if he'd be interested in cunnilingus, and he suddenly he decided to try it. They both knew that he wasn't changing teams, but he wanted to have the experience so he could say he did it once. A classic Sagittarius move.

The Archer is casual and likes to get right to the point. He won't worry about pleasing you because he's more into the experience, so you may have to speak up and let him know what you need. Sagittarius is not necessarily a stud in bed, but he's enthusiastic and likes to do the deed, so you'll forgive him for his less than fabulous skills.

Even if you're not completely satisfied, you'll be back in bed with the Sagittarius man in no time. He has a way about him, and you'll find he can talk you into anything. The Sagittarius male was the one in high school talking the girls out of their virginity.

Sagittarius is open-minded, and if he finds you too prudish, he will simply keep it moving in search of a partner who is able to keep up with him. But if you want to have a lot of fun with a partner who'll do anything you can think of in the bedroom, or the kitchen, or the driveway, or the park, then the Sagittarius is the one for you.

Sagittarius Turn-Ons

- Pull him into a closet during a party.
- Foot massages.
- Lot and lots of sex.
- Foreplay, including lots of oral pleasure.
- Excitement and danger.
- Wear gloves and shoes.
- Oil your body and rub it against him.
- Group sex.
- Sex in the great outdoors.
- Oral and anal sex.
- Join the mile high club.

Moving On Without Drama

If you're bored with the Sagittarius male, chances are he is bored with you. But if you'd prefer him to be the one to leave, it's just a question of making yourself even more boring. Getting a Sagittarius man to leave is not really all that difficult.

Decide that everything you want to do can be done at home, and get mad if he tries to get you to go out. He will undoubtedly go out without you, and that's when you start accusing him of cheating—not that he'll feel bad about it even if he is. Sagittarius thinks that's just what men do. What will bother him is the fact that you're trying to keep tabs on him. Sagittarius needs his freedom as much as the rest of us need air to breathe. Try to control him by demanding that he stop drinking, smoking, gambling or any other activity he considers normal, and he'll start to feel like a caged animal.

If by some strange chance he sticks around even after you've become a homebody, make him regret his choice. Talk constantly about yourself, but with no confidence. He'll cringe when you ask insecure questions like "Does this outfit make me look fat?" When he refers to current events, pretend to be ignorant. Be critical about his job, his clothing, his friends, and his pet. Lose interest in everything that he is passionate about.

Speaking of passion, it's easy to make a Sagittarius lose interest in sex with you. Stop going to the gym. Your inactivity will bother him, and he'll notice the moment you gain your first pound. Start biting your nails and take no interest in your appearance, and he'll be quickly turned off, especially since he's probably already been admiring some hot young thing who just started working in his office.

The only method not recommended for turning off a Sagittarius is to make him think that you're cheating on him. It'll only make him suggest a threesome. Other than that, it doesn't take much effort on your part before he's itching to move on. Chances are there is some woman dying to take your place, and Sagittarius already has her cell number. That sound you hear will be your Sagittarius slamming the door on his way out to the waiting car of a potential lover.

Compatibility

SAGITTARIUS

Sagittarius Man/Aries Woman

This is a hot and ready-to-go couple. Happy to try new things in the bedroom, these two love to keep it moving. Quickies seem to work best, since they always have to be some place other than where they are. If they could just slow down a bit, they might stand a long-term chance.

Even though Aries sometimes craves more attention from her Sagittarius partner, she knows he is not the type she can tie down. He likes things easy. He is a freedom-loving spirit and appreciates Aries giving him room to fly. And why wouldn't she, when she wants her own freedom just as much?

Sagittarius is always ready for a night of passion. It is the one thing that will slow his busy self down. But once the screams of ecstasy are heard, his attention is somewhere else. He has an easygoing nature, but it's also always going . . . somewhere else. Long-term, this relationship may last, but perhaps only if the Sagittarius and Aries don't mind feeling lonely.

Sagittarius Man/Taurus Woman

Taurus will find she loves the Sagittarius man's easygoing, fun spirit. But what she will find a bit challenging is his desire to be admired by others. She will have to keep things spicy in the bedroom to keep his attention focused on her.

Sex is exciting and can encompass a few toys, although Taurus should check with her Sag man before she decides to lash him a few times with that whip she just purchased. Now, new positions, however, are a given. In fact, they are to be expected from the Sagittarius man, so Taurus should take her vitamins and be ready to go and go and go. And she should feel free to lavish him with as much sincere praise as she can.

This duo can work. As long as both partners have plenty of energy, they might make this last for a while. It's just a matter of transferring that sexual excitement and commitment to fun to their life outside the bedroom.

Sagittarius Man/Gemini Woman

This is the easy and breezy duo. Sexually, they complement each other well.

Remember that Gemini is a twin. For other signs, this is not always easy to deal with, but for the Sagittarius man, this will only heighten his enjoyment. After all, how often do you get invited to a ménage a trois? The adventurous Sagittarius will be turned on by the challenge of Gemini's unpredictable personalities.

Neither are the jealous type, which works well, since they both crave attention from the opposite sex. It is easy for each to understand where their partner is and what they need. As long as they don't grow complacent and take their easy fit for granted, this could be a promising, long-lasting relationship.

Sagittarius Man/Cancer Woman

Sex or relationship? That is the question. How can a Sagittarius man enjoy his need for freedom when all his Cancer mate wants is to build a home and feel secure with her mate? He can't. Sag's nature is to be one with the world, taking in new people and opportunities. Cancer could come home every night, curl up with her mate and be at peace.

So, sex sounds like the ticket for these two. Sagittarius will take Cancer to places she's only read about or seen in movies. But a Cancer woman must remember that just because sex is great and feels like it could lead to something more permanent, it might not be the same for Sagittarius. For him, it's a sport with passion. Cancer should be careful not to get caught up in the feeling. Once she becomes possessive, she'll send him running. Her cries of ecstasy will become screams of anger. This combination is not a good idea at all.

Sagittarius Man/Leo Woman

If you're invited to a party thrown by a Sagittarius and his Leo mate, don't walk, run. Passion, fun and fireworks are inevitable with this couple.

In or out of the bedroom, there is nothing insecure about this duo. Sex will be physical. They will experience new sexual positions and make their bodies do things some people would never even imagine possible. The good thing is both Sag and Leo are game to try them. Their egos enjoy being able to send each other to new sexual heights. Sagittarius is secure enough to let Leo take the lead in bed. This submissive role excites him to the hilt, which, of course, excites her, and the volume is turned up another notch.

Clear their schedules, because once these two fires signs get started, they can expect to get busy several times a day for several hours. This kind of sex is not limited to their bedroom. You might hear moaning coming from a public bathroom, their car, their friend's car . . . you get the idea.

A long-term union is definitely a possibility with these two. If they're looking for marriage, they should look no further.

Sagittarius Man/Virgo Woman

Sex will not be what likely keeps this duo together. It's pleasant and enjoyable, but who wants pleasant sex? Well, Virgo does—or at least that's her nature. She will get wild with her Sag partner, but he might have to crack her protective shell first.

This will eventually get old. Sagittarius is always ready to keep the party going. For him, wild and adventurous sex is one way to do it. Between the two, sex can be a push and pull experience. It will be Sag's job to do the pushing and the pulling, getting her to let go and just go sex crazy. There's magic waiting for them once they do.

She, on the other hand, will need to take time to enjoy her new sexual freedom without thinking about where or what she's off to do next.

Unfortunately, the harder Sag has to work to get them on the same page, the harder it will be for him to remain faithful. As far as a long-term relationship, the chances are slim.

Sagittarius Man/Libra Woman

Fun with no boundaries describes this couple. Libra will be open to Sagittarius's sexual adventures, and he is open and willing to show his inner feelings. He's easygoing and she's laid back. They love to be loved, and are not concerned with where things are going for the two of them. Each allows the other to be his or herself with no judgment.

Libra has a huge love of all things beautiful, and Sag enjoys dressing up to please her. Spending money on things they like is a hobby for them. There's never a concern about where the next dollar is coming from, but it seems to come.

This is a fun and outgoing couple who love the idea of hanging out with well-known people. They are pleasure people and can expect to be very happy together for as long as it lasts—possibly a lifetime.

Sagittarius Man/Scorpio Woman

As much as Scorpio wants to dominate her Sagittarius man, she can forget about it. She wants so badly to change him, but she can't tie him up, unless it's for hot and steamy sex. He needs to be able to fly when desired. If she continues to try to control him, he will continue to resist.

Sex with this couple varies from light and fun to wild and crazy, depending on who's taking the lead. For Sagittarius, sex is sex, and for Scorpio, she wants it to go deeper. To her, sex means there is a commitment in the works, but Sag isn't making any promises.

Scorpio can have a strong temper, and when she doesn't get her way, she may lash out and say some not so nice things to her Sag man. He's been known to find her tantrums funny, and his laughter may force her into laughing and lightening up. Who knows? Maybe he could get her to loosen up and the two of them could live happily ever after.

Sagittarius Man/Sagittarius Woman

Fun, fun, fun. Put Sagittarius and Sagittarius together, and that is what it equals.

Sexually, these two can do it all over the place and probably don't mind adding others to bring some extra spice to the union. They will enjoy new places and experience new ways to keep it exciting.

These Sagittarians like their independence, and as a couple, neither wants to give that up. They are always on the go, and barely spend time with each other, though they do like to travel together, taking in new worldly experiences. They are both spiritual and find the subject fascinating.

These two can bring out the worst in each other, so they work toward having an emotion-free relationship. It's better for them when things are light and fun. They both like to laugh a lot, and humor is another important aspect to this couple. Lots of fun these two will have, but we know it takes more than a few laughs to sustain a relationship.

Sagittarius Man/Capricorn Woman

Sagittarius sweeps Capricorn onto her back with a romantic journey she'll never forget—and orgasms that take her to new sexual heights. In the midst of the bump and grind, Capricorn allows herself to let go, clear her mind and ride out the sexual adventure she's been blessed to experience.

When the bedroom doors open, the free spirit sex kitten takes on a new personality. She's back to climbing the ladder to success. What Capricorn demands, Sagittarius can't deliver. They both have big aspirations and very different ways of achieving. All work and no play makes Capricorn a dull girl. And all play and no work makes Sagittarius a man without money.

These signs have two different ideas, two different approaches, one result: friendship.

Sagittarius Man/Aquarius Woman

Sex is good. Real good. Aquarius is ecstatic with Sagittarius's adventurous appetite for sex. Sag is excited because he's met someone who will allow him to exercise his salacious sexual palette. Sagittarius loves to experiment.

Sex will be hot and imaginative, with lots of new things to discover. Lightning has struck here. There are no boundaries with them. They can go from friends to couple, and they will enjoy all the in-between.

They both live life on the edge; two carefree people who live life in the moment. Commitment is not on their agenda, and neither is being faith-

ful to the other. The good thing is, they are both
okay with that. As unconventional as it seems,
this one could actually work.

Sagittarius Man/Pisces Woman

This is another mix-matched duo. They are
pretty much headed toward failure before they
really get started. Sex will be good and there will
be no lack of orgasms; however, try to move this
relationship from sex to love . . . Not!

Pisces is way too emotional for her Sagittarius
partner. She will grow tired of feeling as if her
purpose is to help him develop some emotions.
And as far as he's concerned, all the discussions
about feelings are taking away from the time
for more sex. She's a risk taker, he's not, and if
it weren't for sex, they would have no reason to
stay together.

So, if you're a Pisces woman dating a Sag man
and there's seems to be a mutual attraction, I'd
think twice. Unless you're just in it to hit it, forget about it.

Famous Sagittarius Men

NOVEMBER 22–DECEMBER 21

Jamie Foxx—December 13, 1967
Jay-Z—December 4, 1969
Don Cheadle—November 29, 1964
Robert Guillaume—November 30, 1927
The Game—November 29, 1979
Richard Pryor—December 1, 1940
Mos Def—December 11, 1973
Samuel L. Jackson—December 21, 1948
Tyson—December 19, 1970

Capricorn

December 22–January 19

Your Capricorn Man

If you're looking for a no nonsense tower of strength who will never send you to the poor-house, then you can bet all your money on a Capricorn. Oh, and whatever you do, please don't let him know if you are a closet shopaholic.

Capricorn is a brother who takes financial security seriously and won't respect any individual who is frivolous and wastes money. If you drive a flashy car where the sticker price alone would impress most men, the Capricorn will immediately explain to you the downside of spending two hundred thousand dollars on a car. He'll also help you to see that the resale value is nil because nobody will want to spend that kind of money on a used car. He'll then inform you of all the smart ways you could have invested that money to make more money. And as soon as you walk away, he'll whisper "idiot" under his breath. He hates waste, flash and bling.

But don't be confused. This brother isn't afraid of wealth. In fact, if you get a look at his financial reports, you'll learn he has a diverse portfolio and knows more about the stock market and IRAs than your accountant. He's a sophisticated sort who likes to live well and won't mind working hard to get there. Let me rephrase that: The Capricorn will expect to work hard for whatever he has in life, and he doesn't trust things that come to easily to him, including women. The Capricorn's motto should be "Things worth having are those worth working hard for."

The Capricorn man is well turned out, but you won't see him in flashy or trendy gear. He likes his clothing to be classic and of the highest quality. The kind of clothes that never go out of style. To him, buying the trendiest clothing is wasting money, so he's sticking to traditional gear. But all you fashionistas out there can relax. Traditional doesn't mean outdated or corny. This brother carefully chooses his attire based on the need to put his best foot forward. He's too smart to let his clothing date him by wearing things that played out a long time ago. Capricorn men dress to impress, and they have a definite swagger about them.

When I think of Capricorn men, Denzel Washington, one of the sexiest brothers on the planet comes to mind. Everything about Denzel exudes class, confidence, strength and style. He's a hard-earning, hard-living family man who has been married for almost twenty-five years.

Capricorn may take a long time choosing a mate, but once he does, he is hard pressed to give her up.

While Denzel is often in the spotlight, most Capricorns don't like to be there. This is the least attention-seeking sign in the zodiac. Capricorn is neither a follower nor a leader. He generally prefers his own company to that of a large crowd. Unless it has to do with work, he doesn't want to be in large groups, and if his mate tries to force it, he'll be cranky and annoyed.

Part of the reason Capricorn doesn't like to be around many people is that he believes most people are not who they pretend to be. He has no patience for phonies or posers. Besides, he is close to his friends and family, so he doesn't need to fill up his life with more people than he can give attention to. Chances are he has only one or two close friends whom he trusts, and he's known them forever. Even his best friends know, however, never to drop by unannounced. Capricorn values privacy and is usually so busy being productive that he doesn't have time for socializing.

When it comes to advice, this is the sign most likely to help—sometimes offering his opinion even when you don't want to hear it. If you're looking for a man who will always agree with you, then keep walking past the Capricorn. If you are confused about something and don't know the right thing to do, then you need to ask a Cap. He has high morals, which will factor into making good decisions and doing the right thing.

Second only to Scorpio, the Capricorn will tell it like it is and not worry about you getting your feelings hurt. Capricorn has such a hard time lying that he often suffers from the legendary Capricorn flaw called "foot in mouth disease." He is quick to speak his mind, often forgetting that everyone is not thick-skinned enough to deal with his honesty. He won't tiptoe around the fact that your brother needs to get up off your mama's couch and get his act together, and if your brother ever asks for advice, Capricorn won't hold his tongue.

When he's being honest, he's not trying to be mean. Still, Capricorn is often accused of being cold. But take it easy on the painfully honest Capricorn. It's not his fault that he sees things as they are and not as people would like them to be. There is a life to be managed, and he's about the business of doing just that. So, if you want to get your life together and can handle some brutally honest advice, this is the brother to ask for help.

Just don't expect him to be helpful when he's in a bad mood. When the Capricorn is down, he'll disappear, preferring to suffer in silence. There is no need for an audience to validate him when he's depressed, especially since it doesn't usually last long. He often suffers because he takes on more than he should, which forces him to have to work around the clock. He is extremely capable, and doesn't see a point in slowing down until he has to. When he does finally slow down, he'll need to be alone, but only for a while. It might be frustrating for his mate when he becomes unavailable, but the great thing is that even when he is sad or mad, he won't take it out on anyone else. He always takes full responsibility for his life and how he is feeling.

In love, the Capricorn brother wants a woman who allows him to be vulnerable. He doesn't like being suspicious and serious all the time. He wants to loosen up and have fun. So if you're the type who can handle a strong, confident brother and you can keep it real with him, then this is the one to pursue. I can guarantee that you will never go in the poor house. The Capricorn knows how to keep himself together and to take care of you and the kids, and to inspire you to do even better than you thought you could.

Let's Get It Started

If you're feeling a Capricorn man and want to get to know him better, the number one rule is to be yourself. I mean be your best classy, put-together self, but not phony. Don't make him think you're only putting on a show for him. Capricorn can smell a fake, so it's best to be who you really are. This is a suspicious person, and if you come on too strong, he'll assume you're hiding something.

He likes a woman who dresses like a woman, so instead of showing up in a pair of loafers, put on those sexy heels and a form-fitting dress. Just don't choose the one with the sequins and the barely-there back. Capricorn wants his date to be well turned out, but not flashy. He isn't an attention seeker, and neither should the woman in his life be one.

Whatever outfit you choose, don't let him think you spent an entire paycheck on it. Find a way to casually mention that although it's an expensive designer dress, you bought it on sale. Capricorn craves all kinds of security, but none more than financial. He may date a sister who is bad with her money, but there is no way he'll have any interest in taking her to the altar—no matter how sexy or fabulous she is. If you are piss poor and have no interest in making a solid living, then this is not the man for you.

Capricorn already knows that he immediately improves a woman's life, but he will only consider marrying someone who won't lower the quality of his life by spending all his hard-earned money. He wants to know that you will work as a team to better your futures.

Actually, he wants to know everything about you before he makes any real decisions about your chances as a couple. Don't be surprised if you feel like you're being interrogated by your Capricorn. He can't help it; he's just naturally curious. Just be careful what you tell him about yourself. He has high morals, so if you did some shady stuff, either express remorse or keep it to yourself. Don't bother to lie because he can read body language, and he'll write you off as a loser. Just be yourself, and as long as you are charming, trustworthy and interesting, you'll have a chance.

Along with your financial status, he wants to know that you are interesting and intelligent. Even if you're on a different political side, give him well-thought out facts and he'll respect your opinion, even if it's not his. But make sure you know your subject well. Capricorn is the kind of man who reads several newspapers a day, so you must stay informed about current events and politics. If you usually just skim the headlines and can't carry on an in-depth discussion, then don't bring up the subject because he will figure out quickly that you are only doing it to try to impress him. Unless he feels you are a good intellectual match, he'll never consider you more than friend material.

If you and your Capricorn are ready for that first date, suggest an activity that will stimulate his mind. Capricorn likes the arts, so let him know you have an interest in cultural activities: theater, dance and music. Invite him to a play or a concert. Don't even think about suggesting the hottest nightclub or a crowded, trendy restaurant. Capricorn does not like a crowd, so if you're the type of woman who wants to hang out in these places, then the two of you are not a good match at all. Capricorn likes things low-key.

He is also a brother who likes being catered to, so this is a good time to work your magic by pulling out all the stops. If you're a sister who can cook, show the Cap your skills in the kitchen, and you'll see the wheels turning as he upgrades you to a long-term possibility. This is even more likely to happen after you've gotten to know him better and you invite his family over to enjoy a meal with the two of you.

If you've passed all his tests and his family gives the stamp of approval, you could well be on your way to something serious with the Capricorn. Give yourself a pat on the back for making it this far. When a Capricorn male is ready to take it to the next level with you, it goes without saying that you are the cream of the crop.

Keeping Him Happy

- Let him see that you are smart with money.
- Show him your skills in the kitchen.
- Have your priorities straight.
- Stimulate his mind.
- Spend lots of time with his family.
- Always keep your looks together.
- Never be crass.
- Keep his secrets and respect his privacy.
- Be generous with your affections—in private.
- Demonstrate high morals and be respectable.

Sex

While the Capricorn man is classy and sophisticated and conservative in most areas of his life, all bets are off when it comes to sex. If you see the buttoned-up Goat in the work environment, you'll never guess that he can be a passionate man who will rock your world in the bedroom.

In order for the Cap to view you as a possible partner, he must first trust you. Knowing a partner is a huge turn-on to a Capricorn because he likes to feel there is the possibility of a love connection later on in the relationship. For the Capricorn, foreplay will include plenty of talk, so don't be afraid to open up to him. Sharing your feelings and your erotic fantasies—as long as you don't use crass or slutty language—will make him feel closer to you, and enhance your lovemaking.

Capricorn likes to be the initiator, so let him decide when he's had enough foreplay and is ready to turn on the heat between you. Once he gets things going, though, you can't just lay there and let him do all the work. As much as he needs to control the pace and experience of sex, he wants to know that you're turned on as well. He is curious to know what works and doesn't work, so talk to him while he's taking care of you. Then when it's your turn, he'll tell you exactly how to excite him. He wants this to be a mutually satisfying experience for both of you.

Capricorn will set the stage with candles, soft lighting, and sexy music. The environment will be comfortable and luxurious, so don't be surprised if he's laid down a bearskin rug in front of the fireplace. You can help him enjoy the sensuous experience by bringing some scented oils to rub him down, and wearing silky, feminine lingerie. Stay away from the crotchless panties and stripper-like attire, though. He always wants his woman to be ladylike, even in the bedroom.

While he wants you to be a lady, it will turn him on immensely if you remind him how much of a man he is. Whisper in his ear how hot he makes you, how good he makes you feel. Don't be shy during oral sex. He will appreciate a woman who shows just how much she loves his manhood by swallowing it eagerly. Capricorn loves to masturbate, so explain that you'd like to watch him and see how turned on he gets. Basically, let him know that you are willing to make his penis the center of your world. Capricorn is a nice guy who happens to want lots of sex, and he wants a partner who can provide as much as he needs. And when he's found her, he's more than happy to make sure she's equally satisfied in the bedroom.

Remember that Capricorn likes to be planning for his future, both in and out of the bedroom. If you've already passed his financial and intelligence tests, and then you show him you're the type of woman who will keep him erect all night long, he might just be ready to propose marriage on the spot.

Capricorn Turn-Ons

- Rub your nipples over his body.
- Lightly flick a feather under his arm.
- Engage his mind by describing your fantasies while you're making love.
- Let him lead.
- Dress in sexy, classy lingerie.
- Include plenty of foreplay.
- Create lavish, sensual surroundings.
- Hold intimate conversation.

Moving On Without Drama

Driving your Capricorn man out the door isn't hard, but once it's done, it is final. So make sure that you really want things to be over before you take these steps.

The Goat despises drama, so the best place to start is to stage a few jealous fits. He is all about security and sensibility. He's not the type to take a day off of work just for the heck of it, so start complaining that he spends more time at his job than with you. Suggest that maybe the reason he is always so eager to go to work is because he's having an affair with his secretary. It's unlikely that the practical Capricorn has ever even considered something as frivolous as a workplace affair, so he'll take great offense to your accusation. Insist on calling his secretary to verify his story with her, and you just might send him over the edge. He won't like you questioning his word, and he certainly won't stand for being embarrassed like that.

Anything that you do to draw negative attention to your Capricorn man will send him a few steps closer to leaving you. Lose your ladylike pencil skirts and heels, and replace them with sloppy, baggy sweats. This sign takes his mate's appearance personally. If you look like a hot mess in public, he will hate that it reflects badly on him. Match your ugly outfits with loud, obnoxious statements in public, and he just might deny even knowing you.

The further he tries to distance himself from you and your low-class behavior, the more clingy you should become.

Whine and ask him why he's such a stick in the mud. Tell him it wouldn't kill him to give you a little kiss or a hug in public once in a while. And come to think of it . . . rattle off a whole list of things about him that you'd like to change. This works especially well if you do it in front of his family members.

If you really want to see some fireworks, start in on his family members. Complain that his mother babies him too much. Try accusing his father of cheating on his mother, and he might put you out before you can even blink.

If you're still around, invite over a few or your own family members that he doesn't like. You know, people like your cousin Lenny, who's always asking to borrow money, even though he hasn't had a job since Bill Clinton was in office and there's no way he'll pay back the loan. Go ahead and give Lenny that money, and while you're at it, tell him to bring a crowd of friends to the house with him. The poor Capricorn prefers to be alone, and he won't be able to handle the combination of your deadbeat cousin and a noisy crowd all under his roof, upsetting his serenity.

Before you know it, your Capricorn is kicking you out the door. He won't stand for his life being a mess, and that includes the woman in it, so bon voyage. See you next lifetime.

Compatibility

CAPRICORN

Capricorn Man/Aries Woman

She's a "whatever, let's just go for it" type, and he is a "I always do it this way" type. So, where does that leave them? Eventually searching for a different relationship.

Their extreme differences will carry over into the bedroom as well. Foreplay for the Capricorn man will consist of a heated discussion on the latest *New York Times* article. The Aries woman would rather skip all the talking and just get down to business. She will find herself frustrated, enduring a discussion about the bank account and her spending habits before any sexual stimulation takes place. If she was hoping for a partner who'll have her hanging upside down, swinging from the chandelier, she can forget it with a Capricorn.

This duo is someone else's idea of a good time.

Capricorn Man/Taurus Woman

This is a practical couple. They mesh together well, though their sexual union is not usually accompanied by lots of fireworks. They both love sex, but there needs to be some thought put into it. This couple's idea of a recipe for great sex is wonderful conversation; before, during and after. Taurus can be a little more free in the bedroom, so she will have to be patient with her Capricorn man and let him take things at his slower, more deliberate pace. He doesn't like to be rushed. If she can handle this, she's sure to enjoy a long, erotic night between the sheets.

This duo might not engage in very adventurous sex, but there is lots of stability in this relationship. Taurus is usually looking for someone to make a sturdy home life with her, and she can feel safe with a Capricorn man, who will always have his eye toward making a good future for them. Together, their lives are simple, safe and sensible.

Capricorn Man/Gemini Woman

Don't put too much stock in this union lasting. Capricorn and Gemini are an unlikely pair.

Even if they feel some initial chemistry, these two will constantly bump heads. Gemini loves to run with life and play. Capricorn is very busy at work; he only runs for fitness. These two work better as buddies or confidants.

When sex between the two happens, it will be enjoyable. The intense Gemini might be able to convince Capricorn to loosen up and let out a few hollers. If he gets caught up, he might even roll over and give Gemini a sexy spanking. Gemini should keep a list of things that will make him laugh, and just before they're ready to get busy, lay a few jokes or funny stories on him. It'll make the transition from uncontrollable laughter to uncontrollable sex a little more likely to happen. This is when it's a good time slip in a few new sexual positions. Who knows? He might like them so much that they become a permanent part of their sex nights.

Long-term, Gemini is looking for a solid man, one that is a good citizen. She can find that in a Capricorn man. However, her free spirit will wear on him after a while, as will the unpredictability of her twin nature. I predict short-term or no-term for this duo.

Capricorn Man/Cancer Woman

What do you get when you put together the emotional Cancer with the all-business Capricorn? A train wreck. These two are both homebodies, but in very different ways. Cancer's home is a place where she goes after work to retreat, take care of her man, cook great meals, have great sex and take a soothing bubble bath. Capricorn's home is a place where he keeps a second desk to finish the work he brought home.

Sex will be nurturing; Cancer will see to that. But to the Capricorn, it might also feel dutiful. He will be expected to shower his Cancer mate with affection, and will have to read her mind to figure out what she needs. It's not in her nature to just come out and tell him, which is exactly what Capricorn wants.

While their relationship might not be passionate, Capricorn will treat his Cancer woman with respect. He will always protect her reputation because he knows she has worked hard for it and he understands that once it's damaged, she can't get it back. She's an old fashioned girl who likes to keep it simple. Unfortunately, she's also very sensitive, and after a while, Capricorn's tendency to offer his opinion will prove to be more than she can handle. This couple is not expected to enjoy anything long-term.

Capricorn Man/Leo Woman

Egos run the show when these two get together. These same egos are what will provoke a
very hot and steamy sex night. Neither Capricorn
nor Leo will want to be outdone by the other.

When one is ready for sex, the other will always feel the need to oblige. This is great if a Leo
woman can turn on her desire no matter what is
going on in her life, but if not, it creates a lot of
pressure to continually perform. They will convince themselves that the sex act is love-driven,
but in reality it is often a sort of competition.
The more sexual excitement they can muster up,
screaming and moaning, the more it will demonstrate to the other one that they mean business.

Their greatest challenge will be outside the
bedroom. Leo loves to be in the spotlight, while
Capricorn prefers not to be the center of attention. While he wants to stay home and carry on
meaningful conversations with his mate, Leo
wants to be out on the town, basking in the spotlight. Aside from sexual chemistry, these two will
find that they have very little in common. They
should enjoy a few fun nights together and leave
it at that.

Capricorn Man/Virgo Woman

Talk about a couple with potential. Their sexual bond is strong. Their sex is both mental and physical, and they approach everything in their lives the same way. Capricorn and Virgo are workaholics and have plans for how most of their lives will run, even in the bedroom. They will be on the same page when it comes to planning out the exact nature of every sexual encounter, every last detail, before it even takes place. An evening in the hot tub together means just that, and these two won't make other plans or expect more.

Capricorn and Virgo are both family-oriented, so neither will mind that they spend much of their time with relatives. They are also practical with money and share many of the same values, so the probability of fighting over finances is pretty low. Together, this duo can accomplish just about anything they put their minds to, and that includes sexing each other up until they reach the most mind-blowing orgasms. Some people find it boring to play it safe, but not these two. A long-lasting relationship filled with lots of love and respect is inevitable.

Capricorn Man/Libra Woman

Libra loves affection, which means she'll have a hard time with the Capricorn, who tends to bury his emotional needs. When Capricorn focuses on work, he is concerned with securing a future. It could mean he thinks the relationship is heading toward marriage. But Libra might get tired of him being distracted and distant, and she'll bolt before they have a chance to go deeper.

Sexually, they are both initiators, and they have a lustful appetite for nights of hot, passionate sex. Libra is drawn to Capricorn's strong sexuality. He should try to remember, though, that she wants romance and flowers. She likes it when her mate pays attention and flatters her. Unfortunately, Capricorn is most likely working or too busy achieving to notice. And when he does, his affections are so wound up inside, he's unable to share them with her.

Libra will not tolerate this for very long. She can try to convince Capricorn that love is not just a commitment, but an opportunity to be open and emotional. If she's successful, she might wind up deeply satisfied. And if the Cap can teach her to value the almighty dollar and to keep away from SALE signs, this might make it past a week—but probably not much more.

Capricorn Man/Scorpio Woman

This water sign woman and earth sign man complement each other both in and out of the bedroom.

Sexually, they are a good match. She loves to be on top during sex, but doesn't mind stepping back and letting Capricorn take the lead when he wants. He spends so much time working, though, that when it's play time, he might not mind striking a laid back pose and letting this sister whip it on him. He uses sex as a stress reliever, which she is happy to assist him with. His sex drive is not as active as hers, but this woman has tricks to get him in the mood whenever and wherever.

Capricorn is a calming anchor for Scorpio's sometimes volatile emotions. She can be possessive, but is only trying to express her deep feelings for him. Scorpio is comfortable enough to let her love show, although it is sometimes too over-the-top. When she's in one of her unreasonable moods, she will realize that Capricorn doesn't care that much about them, and she'll learn to rein them in a bit.

His focus is on how to make money and secure a name for himself in the world. It's important for Capricorn to provide a good life for his family. If Scorpio could get him to pay a bit more attention to her, things would pretty much be perfect. They both take their relationship seriously. Scorpio knows that when you catch a Capricorn, it's for life. So with some tweaking, they could be saying "I do" in no time.

Capricorn Man/Sagittarius Woman

Well, imagine getting wild and crazy on the dance floor and your partner has two left feet. That describes Capricorn and Sagittarius.

These two can never seem to get on the same page. His sexual positions consist of the ones he has grown comfortable with, and the Sagittarius, she's a break-dancer. She's up for the new, and new things only distract him. He's comfortable with routines and actually functions best with things in order. Routine for Sagittarius is like a death row sentence. She will spend money for pleasure, and Capricorn saves money for pleasure. He's not a big party-goer like Sagittarius. While he prefers intimate evenings with friends and family or alone, she's somewhere in the middle of a dance floor having a good time. He's the eater, she exercises.

To Capricorn, Sagittarius is wasting precious time on useless activities. Sagittarius doesn't understand why he won't relax and live a bit. With all these differences, it's a miracle when a Capricorn and Sagittarius make it past a one-night stand. And if they do, you might ask yourself, why bother? Because we always feel that we can change the other person.

Don't believe it. These two should just move on. Save themselves.

Capricorn Man/Capricorn Woman

Two Capricorns are well matched sexually. They may from time to time yell out a few animal noises when the sex gets good. But in order to really let go, they would need someone other than another Capricorn to help unleash their inner freak.

Outside the bedroom, they revert back to their more reserved Capricorn nature. You would think they didn't know dating was supposed to be fun. Foreplay for them might consist of watching CNN and having a discussion about it. He might fondle her breast as she finishes the *Wall Street Journal*. They are cautious, reserved, serious people who don't waste time on frivolous things. They are all work and very little play. If they do play, I'm sure it's done with a touch of elegance.

If either had a more carefree mate, they could let their hair down and have fun, but together, everything is by the book. No risks are taken with these two. They do what they know and leave it at that, and eventually, this will be one big snooze fest.

Capricorn Man/Aquarius Woman

Sex will be ambitious, but they will clash big time in the bedroom—and in every other room. These are strong personalities.

Aquarius needs to be free, but Capricorn wants to dominate. He is a by-the-book, follow-the-rules kind of guy, while she makes and breaks her own rules. Aquarius likes to be out in the world, having fun and spending money. That new dress, a vacation, or a fine restaurant: if she makes the money, she should spend it. When she's not spending on herself, the humanitarian Aquarius is helping others. On the other hand, Cap believes that God helps those who help themselves.

Capricorn tries to impose strict control over Aquarius and her frivolous ways. Unless she slows down and learns to be more responsible or he accepts her free-spirited, wasteful lifestyle, there will be no need to pursue this relationship any longer, because it's headed down an icy hill.

Capricorn Man/Pisces Woman

Capricorn will find the Pisces woman understanding and comforting. Pisces will find the Capricorn man solid and dependable. This romance is grounded.

The incredible sex tends to get better as the bond between them grows stronger. He's lustful in the bedroom, and she likes to drive him wild. She's ultra feminine, and the Capricorn is all masculine. They fulfill each other's fantasies of what the opposite sex is supposed to be. He wants her to bring on any fantasy she's ever had. He's ready to fulfill her sexual needs.

These are two very different personalities who meet each other's needs. Pisces works well with Capricorn's strong personality. She feels secure and loves that he takes charge and makes decisions. She doesn't complain when Capricorn is focused on work, because she is able to see the long-term benefits of his workaholic nature. Capricorn loves how Pisces's romantic senses and idealism complement his serious approach to life.

For the sake of longevity, Capricorn should not rely on Pisces's money management skills. This is one of the few places where they could be headed for disaster. If he keeps her spending under control, Capricorn can make the Pisces's dreams into reality. If each of them is looking for real love and is willing to compromise on a few personality differences, this union is promising.

Famous Capricorn Men

DECEMBER 22–JANUARY 19

John Legend—December 28, 1978
Dallas Austin—Dec. 29, 1979
Daniel Sunjata—December 30, 1971
Denzel Washington—December 28, 1954
Tyrese—December 30, 1978
LL Cool J.—January 14, 1968
Ray-J—January 17, 1981
Taye Diggs—January 2, 1971
Steve Harvey—January 17, 1956
Rockman Dunbar—January 11, 1973
Shawn Wayans—January 19, 1971
John Amos—December 27, 1939
Duane Martin—January 1, 1970
Cuba Gooding—January 2, 1968
Doug E. Doug—January 7, 1970
Mekhi Phifer—December 29, 1974

Aquarius

January 20–February 18

Your Aquarius Man

The Aquarius man is an inventor, and he's always looking to create something new and different. While other signs are content with the status quo, the Water Bearer dances to the beat of his own drum, and that means he's going to live in the world exactly as he wants. He's not going to do things like his parents or siblings, and certainly not the way he learned in school. This man is all about new ideas and changing the way the world works. To the Aquarius brother, once something has already been done and perfected, there is no reason to keep doing it that way. He is always thinking outside the box.

Aquarius is the sign of the humanitarian, so behind everything he does is the desire to help those less fortunate than himself. See, he knows that he can do anything he sets his mind to, but he's not sure everybody else is aware that they have the same power, and so his life's mission is using his knowledge and passion to create opportunity for everyone. If the Aquarius goes into the field of medicine, there is a huge chance he'll enter the field of research, where he can find cures for cancers and diseases that others might think impossible. Most look at him as a visionary because he thrives on uncharted territory and has no interest in playing it safe.

Unfortunately, the Aquarius is the friend of the zodiac, which means he is everybody's best friend, so you won't have his full attention for long. He can't help that he is a people person, and though he has plenty of friends, many of them will admit that they don't often feel like they know him that well. The Aquarius can have a hard time expressing his feelings, especially if he was hurt when he was younger.

The Aquarius is often accused of being cold and distant when people first meet him. He's simply got so many ideas swarming around in his head he's probably trying to rush off and write them down. He's also vulnerable, and doesn't want anyone to know that. I guarantee if you have an Aquarius mate and he reads this, he'll be completely uncomfortable and deny that this accurately describes him. If you know him well, you'll agree with him just to let him off the hook, even though you think it's true. It's important you let him believe he's gotten away with his armor intact.

Aquarius is not someone who needs to go deep with many people. If he has a mate, he'll tell her most things—except those that involve other women. The opposite sex adores the Aquarius, even if they have a hard time understanding him. He enters romantic relationships through the doorway of friendship. Those friendships probably have benefits, but that's not necessary in order for him to bond with a sister. He likes to know everything about a woman before he gets involved with her. Often the woman has let go of any thoughts of being with him by the time he finally decides to express his affection. He is a man full of surprises.

The Aquarius can usually see the gifts and creativity of others, which probably accounts for his popularity. People like having a psychic friend around, who they can trust with their secrets. Aquarius is not someone who will share his buddy's indiscretions with anyone, including his significant other. But just because an Aquarius man refuses to talk about his cheating friend or pass judgment on him doesn't mean you have to worry that your Aquarius will do the same.

This is the sign of the individual.

The Water Bearer is not a follower, and in fact, he can't find any reason to copy another person when there are so many undiscovered ways to do everything. He wants to make a difference in the world, and feels he can best do that by being an individual. He is not afraid to be seen as weird or eccentric. In fact, he prefers people to acknowledge that he is an individual and not doing the same old things the same old ways. If they think that makes him a freak or arrogant, oh well.

Aquarius has little respect for people who have to stick to the status quo. If you want to get an Aquarius riled up, tell him that something can't be done. The Aquarius will immediately set about trying to prove you wrong, and thank you for the challenge, even if you didn't mean it that way.

He can see the upside to almost any experience, and wants others to view life that way also. Aquarius likes for everyone to be happy. He is not in the least bit jealous of the success of others and can't imagine hating on others, no matter how lucky they may be. The Aquarius will just keep on stepping, secure in his belief that he has the power within him to achieve the same things if he so chooses. Some people might resent Aquarius for this happy-go-lucky personality, but he is just being himself. This brother is one hundred percent real, and won't waste any time on superficial people.

Part of the reason he can't stand fake people is because Aquarius is truly interested in what's on the inside. He's not overly impressed by a person's wealth, and is incapable of treating people differently based on their social or financial status. To him, money is not what defines a person.

This is not to say, however, that Aquarius doesn't like to have money. In fact, he loves to have it because it affords him the freedom to live the way he chooses. Aquarius is terrified of being tied down, and having an adequate supply of money means he can change plans midstream—change jobs or move across the country, perhaps—and still be okay.

If you are creative and like to try the unknown, then you have found a good match in an Aquarius. He will be generous and kind, and allow you to explore and grow on your own. He might even lend you a few self-help and new-age books from his own collection. The free-spirited, free-thinking Aquarius gives everything in his relationships, and will know how to get you to the next stage of your life, sometimes in exciting new ways you never even dreamed of.

Let's Get It Started

If you have your sights set on an Aquarius man, then the first thing you must do is make yourself stand out from the crowd of women surrounding this friendly, fun-loving brother. While he enjoys the attention of all these ladies, he prefers a woman who can be an individual. Instead of wearing some version of the little black dress that every woman has in her closet, put on something that expresses your individuality. Accent your outfit with a brightly colored, unique scarf you bought on a trip through Europe. Not only will it set you apart, but it will be a great conversation starter, a way for you to fill him in on your adventurous side.

Safe is boring to the Aquarius, so let him know you're a risk-taker. If you quit a desk job to go on that trip to Europe, and you backpacked your way solo across the continent, you'll gain his respect. If you took the trip as part of a guided tour and never strayed away from the guide to explore the countryside on your own, don't mention those details to the Aquarius. He won't consider you mate material if you're the type who's afraid to step outside of the typical mold.

If you start to tell him about your ten-year plan, neatly thought out with lots of dependable investments that guarantee a safe and secure future, this brother will have to stop himself from yawning in your face. Instead, share your most extreme dream about wanting to fly planes or dedicate your summers to the Peace Corps, and you'll have his attention.

He loves women who are passionate and fearless about their desires and dreams. It's an added bonus if your dreams include helping other people. It's okay to dream of being fabulously wealthy, as long as part of your desire is to give half of your wealth to a worthy charity. The Aquarius is a true humanitarian and wants to be involved in positive change in the world around him. If you're involved in any causes or science that will make an impact on the world, let the brother know, and you'll be promoted to the head of the class.

Of course, this doesn't mean he'll kick everyone else to the curb completely. If you want to be with this brother then you need to get your social butterfly tuned up. He needs a partner who can be in the world, hanging with his constant stream of friends. Aquarius is definitely not interested in the kind of homebody with a "you and me against the world" attitude. No matter how committed his relationship, he doesn't ever want to be told that he can't go hang with his friends, even if some of them are female. He makes friends easily and often loses his way home at night because he's run into a few more acquaintances. If you truly have your heart set on an Aquarius man, be prepared to suppress any jealous instincts you may have.

Now, even if you have captivated the Aquarius with your conversation and your individuality, you won't know for sure if he's feeling you. The Aquarius doesn't give much away. So it'll probably be on you to suggest a first date. When choosing the location of the date, you must keep a few things in mind about his personality.

Many Aquarians live on the fringe and are artists, musicians, poets, therapists, scientists—those who don't necessarily have to follow rules for a "normal" life. Aquarius is often eccentric and out there, and won't think twice about wearing some loud outfit that doesn't fit in at a conservative function. This isn't a man interested in molding himself to fit anybody else's idea of who he should be. Keep these things in mind when planning your first date with an Aquarius.

He bores easily, so avoid the regular date night themes, like dinner and a movie. For your first date, try inviting him to something intellectual, like a book reading or the theater. And be prepared to bite your tongue if you're the type who might ask "You're wearing that?" Aquarius won't care if you're in a sequined ball gown while he's wearing jeans, so you better not care either.

If you want to take him to dinner after your first date, remember that Aquarius likes romance, so along with the invitation, text him a haiku or email a poem. Share some creativity with him and you'll have his attention. As for the location, think planetarium and picnic under the stars. Or perhaps invite him to an ethnic restaurant, since he likes spices. Indian, Ethiopian, Japanese, Brazilian and Korean are among his favorite foods. At dinner, feed him, and he'll return the favor by licking your fingers and giving you an idea of how good he'll be to you later.

Dinner conversation should not include certain topics. Definitely avoid discussions of marriages and babies, even if every one of your girlfriends has recently gotten married or is pregnant. The idea of settling down frightens him. Aquarius likes to be free to roam the world, and can't easily imagine himself with the house, the white picket fence and the rest of that fantasy.

In fact, if this whole domestic fantasy is what you're looking for in the future, then perhaps you should just ask for the check now and seek out a more compatible sign.

But if you like the idea of being with a free-spirited Aquarius, show him that you have plenty of other things on your mind, like world issues or some fascinating, unusual hobby. Think outside the box. As long as he knows you're not trying to convert him to some cult, he'll be interested in whatever you have to say, especially if you're giving him insight into who you truly are.

Don't bother making things up to impress him. Be yourself, and you'll get a lot further with this brother. If things do progress and he decides you're the one, you might not have a conventional lifestyle, but you will certainly lead an interesting life with your Aquarius man.

Keeping Him Happy

- Give to his favorite charity and show that you're a humanitarian.
- Stimulate his mind with intelligent conversation.
- Buy him books.
- Be easygoing and social.
- Talk about modern technology.
- Make him laugh.
- Give him plenty of space.
- Don't expect routine.
- Don't expect him to conform. Appreciate his individuality.
- Be a true visionary.
- Tell him you love him often.

Sex

When it comes to sex, Scorpio gets all the praise, but it's the Aquarius male who has written all the manuals. Those that he hasn't written, like the Kama Sutra, he's studied cover to cover and memorized every position. He's the master at making love to a woman so that she not only feels satisfied, she feels reborn. Yeah, this is a man who knows exactly what he is doing when it comes to pleasing a woman.

Aquarius is patient, thoughtful and creative. He'll start foreplay, and you can bet you'll have at least one orgasm before he even gets to cunnilingus. The Aquarius will not leave one area of your body unexplored. He'll remind you that your ears are not just for hearing and your toes aren't simply there to be polished. This brother turns it up from the start.

When it comes to sex, Aquarius is absolutely sure about what he wants, and that is to please you. If you tell him you've never had an orgasm, the Aquarius man will not let you out of bed until you've had your fourth climax. He's thoughtful that way, and wants you to have the kind of experience you'll never forget.

Go ahead, tell him what you like. But he won't stop there. He'll expand on your suggestions. If there are any new sex toys on the market to guarantee pleasure, the Aquarius already has them and will wear you out with them. All this is often before he gets down to the business at hand.

Sex is not something he rushes, no matter how much you beg to be entered. He'll get there in his own time. If this is your second or third encounter, you'll notice he never does it the same way twice. The Aquarius is easily bored, so he works to keep his sex life fresh by adding new positions. He wants to have the ultimate sexual experience, and he knows you have to switch it up to get there.

Aquarius is always down for a threesome because he knows he has enough stamina to please any two women. He's not just interested in the two women pleasing him. The biggest part of his pleasure is watching you get off, and if you tell him about a fetish or something really freaky, he won't blink. Instead, he'll do anything you need to turn you on and satisfy you.

Yeah, it's not just sex with Aquarius, it's an entire world. Think of him as an amusement park, and you'll have a good idea what a treat you're in for.

Aquarius Turn-Ons

- The wilder the better.
- Exploring new positions—or creating your own!
- Having sex standing up against a wall.
- Threesomes.
- Running a feather across his penis.
- Sex toys.
- Lingerie.
- Telling him your most outrageous fantasy.
- Tantric sex.
- Letting him give you the full oral pleasure treatment.

Moving On Without Drama

Getting your Aquarius to leave is easy, but chances are you'll still want to be friends. The good news is that you can have both.

The first thing you should do to turn him off is stop being so easygoing. Impose schedules and restrictions on your relationship that were never there before. Make a big deal when he's late for anything, which will happen often. Get pissed if he doesn't make it to dinner each night. Refuse to attend social functions with him, then wait up and ask him how he has the nerve to be staying out so late. Tell him you've given it some thought and you don't like the idea of him going away on vacation with his boys.

Start to act like the most conservative, narrow-minded woman. Watch the political talk-shows and make him think you're starting to agree with the far-right Republicans. Argue against all his liberal ideas. Tell him that everybody, no matter who they are, should be responsible for themselves. Complain bitterly about family members he still supports. Instead of donating to a charity, use your tax return to buy yourself something expensive and unnecessary.

When he wants sex, complain that you've had a headache and wear flannel to bed. Keep your sexual activity very unimaginative, and stick to the missionary position. Your Aquarius man lives to give you orgasms, so if you start having trouble achieving the big O, his ego won't be able to handle it.

But here's the easiest and quickest way to get rid of an Aquarius man: Tell him you're thinking about throwing out your birth control because you want to start a family. Suggest that it's time for him to get a stable, suit-and-tie job so he can support you and a baby. If he already makes a good living, complain that it's not a "normal" job and you want him to do something more mainstream and respectable. You won't believe how fast he's gone once he hears those words.

He'll be off seeking a cooler, more laid back woman to be his partner. But don't worry. This won't be the last time you hear from the Aquarius. Because he is not a judgmental brother, he won't hold your new, uptight nature against you. After all, he wants everyone to be happy and be themselves. He might not agree with your new point of view, but he'll still wish you the best. You can no longer be his woman, but he'll be happy to put you back among the ranks of his many female friends.

Compatibility

AQUARIUS

Aquarius Man/Aries Woman

The Aquarius man is quite the cool one, but, like the Aries woman, he loves and appreciates sexual impulses, passion and great freaky sex. These two will have no problem igniting each other's fire. Aries likes to be on top when she's having sex, and Aquarius won't mind because it'll make him create new positions for them.

Aquarius likes that the Aries female is a different kind of person, not like most women. She is a character, and likes to change personalities as often as she changes clothes. This will keep Aquarius entertained. Both like to be in relationships as long as they don't have to change, and that won't be a problem here.

They can screw each other's brains out and call it love, and who knows? It just might be.

With the interesting combination of sex and friendship, things are never dull with this pair.

Aquarius Man/Taurus Woman

Get out the boxing gloves. These two will duel often, and may the best zodiac sign win.

If they can get past the debates about who is to do what, they can actually enjoy a night between the sheets. Taurus can sometimes be sexually tight and not want to open herself up to such a wild card, but Aquarius makes no apologies about himself, and the Bull finds that sexy. If Taurus can find a way to release herself, Aquarius will offer up a night of passion that will keep her coming back for more.

Outside of the bedroom, these signs are both strong-willed and quite different. Taurus likes to plan things, but Aquarius needs to be spontaneous. And even though Taurus is an amazing homemaker, she shouldn't bother cooking for the Aquarius because by the time he shows up, dinner will be ice cold, and so will the Taurus.

How about we skip this one?

Aquarius Man/Gemini Woman

Aquarius's and Gemini's sexual energies are
more than compatible. Psychic ability seems
heightened with this duo. They can spend an afternoon exploring a few adult shops, and chances
are that because they're so in tune mentally, they
will both pick the same items. They love exploring sex, and they seem able to express sexual
desires without words. Both like experimenting
with new kinds of sex, which means these two
can completely turn each other out.

The Aquarius needs sex in order to feel connected to a woman, and the Gemini needs sex
in order to stay connected to herself. In other
words, they both need a lot of it, and will be more
than happy to provide it for their partner as well.
Sure, they'll fight sometimes, but even that won't
stop them from having incredible sex.

Neither has a problem giving the other space,
since both need lots of freedom. Once they leave
the bedroom, they'll go out and party; sometimes together, sometimes separately. Either
way, they won't have to worry about a jealous
partner pressuring them.

Yeah, this is a keeper because aside from the
fantastic sex, the Aquarius and Gemini duo will
like the idea that they'll always have a road dog.

Aquarius Man/Cancer Woman

Okay, let's start with the sex. It will be fabulous. Aquarius and Cancer are very different signs, but when it comes to sex, they are on point together. The Aquarius man is a freak, and the Cancer woman likes to let loose between the sheets.

Nonetheless, problems will arise. The Aquarius man likes variety and enjoys his freedom, but the Cancer believes she is enough for any man. Cancer's range of emotions and clinginess will send the Aquarius packing or finding other reasons to never come home.

Outside the bedroom, this duo does okay. Both agree that it's important to make a difference in this world, which gives them lots of charities to donate time and money to.

When it comes to work, these two are a good pair. But when it comes to play, one gets bored and the other gets her feelings hurt. This couple works much better as business partners who slip between the sheets every once in a while.

Aquarius Man/Leo Woman

Leo feels like the queen on the throne with this Aquarius man. Sex is an adventure for both of them. Freaky and wild, these two are always ready to roll. On any given night, the incredible passion in their bedroom makes their lovemaking something average couples might pay to watch.

Aquarius flatters the Leo woman with much attention, which makes it easy to fall for him. Leo can almost live on flattery alone. But there will be clashes when it comes to their personalities. Aquarius is an individual, not concerned with outside influences, who desires to change the world. Leo is a bit of a narcissist who only wants to donate to charity if she can be publicly congratulated for her generosity. After all, it's all about her.

If these two can come to a meeting of the minds, they could have a chance for the long-haul. After all, they both live to have fun.

Aquarius Man/Virgo Woman

These two are quite opposite, and unfortunately, their differences will follow them into the bedroom. Virgo likes sex to be normal and calm. Aquarius wants his socks blown off, and it's not going to happen here. Virgo likes to plan it out, and well, only one of them will find that sexy. Aquarius prefers sex to be a rollercoaster of many quirky, outrageous things, and this could be frightening to the thoughtful, careful Virgo. Aquarius will have to work very hard to bring out her passionate side, in and out of the bedroom.

Virgo is easily distracted by thoughts of business or future plans, concepts that can make an Aquarius break out in hives. The Water Bearer likes life to be more spontaneous, and the Virgo likes to keep to a schedule. She isn't interested in going off the beaten path, but the Aquarius isn't happy to keep trudging a road that's been traveled. While the Aquarius appreciates Virgo's commitment to detail, he doesn't want his own life to be so detailed.

These two should stick to being pals.

Aquarius Man/Libra Woman

Aquarius and Libra create an immediate friendship which could lead to a lovely affair. This combination has the makings of a good marriage.

Libra's laid back nature gets a spark when Aquarius brings his experimental kind of love-making. She also brings her own spontaneous joy into the bedroom, taking Aquarius to an emotional level of sex he rarely visits. They have a free approach to sex, and if the need for some freaky stuff rears its head, then so be it.

Their home together is beautiful and calming, and both like to keep a simplicity about their lives. Space is also a prerequisite for this union. He loves to please her, and she loves that about him. And when things don't go as smoothly as she would like, she applauds his efforts.

On the downside, they could find themselves financially in a slump. With Aquarius's thirst for new things and Libra's desire to buy whatever it takes to keep her surroundings beautiful, they will find themselves going through their savings quickly. If they can work out their money issues or maybe hire a financial manager, they could have a long, successful partnership.

Aquarius Man/Scorpio Woman

These are two stubborn people. Aquarius wants to break free and explore; Scorpio wants to prepare a lovely dinner for two at home.

Sex is where it works. He loves to be tied up; perhaps to the bed post, perhaps to the piano. As long as he's in bondage, he can enjoy the thrill of escaping. And the Scorpio woman gets to enjoy the benefits of their playful sexual union.

Even if these two only came together for the sex, they would be greatly satisfied. Scorpio's sexual appetite is stronger than Aquarius's, and that alone fascinates him. She likes it dirty, nasty and often. He can keep up with her and show her a few new tricks. Aquarius likes threesomes, but Scorpio will keep him so entertained he won't even need it.

Out of the bedroom, she makes emotional demands and needs him to commit immediately. He can't move as fast as she wants, which sends her in a rage. Unfortunately, she cannot dominate an Aquarius's casual approach to love and his many outside interests. Scorpio's insecurities will set in after too many nights of unexplained absences. When you think Aquarius, think restless, with emotions buried deep. When you think Scorpio, think jealous and demanding. Not a happy combination.

Oh, if only they could survive on the sex, it would be fantastic.

Aquarius Man/Sagittarius Woman

There's a possibility for a long-lasting relationship with these two. It can move from "Hi, my name is . . ." to "I do" in the blink of an eye.

Aquarius needs an independent woman who is busy with her own life. He needs to be able to move around freely with his many ideas. Sagittarius fits this bill quite well. Rarely do these two stay in the moment. They are both adventurous people and like the ability to explore life and all its wonders.

Sexually, it's the same. There are no inhibitions, and they will try new things just for the sake of not repeating something they've already perfected. Boundaries are limitless with them. They could go at it all night—with each other, or perhaps with someone else.

Faithful? Well, if you mean to their beliefs, they are, one hundred percent. To each other? Not so much. If they were, then they would not be the spontaneous, free-spirited individuals that they are, right?

This is a hot duo, and sex can be off the chain. But long-term, don't expect either of them to be planning for the future. The thing that works with them is that neither one has a problem with that "live for the moment" attitude. If they do hook up, there is always the possibility that they'll sign up for an open marriage.

Aquarius Man/Capricorn Woman

Definitely a rough go of it. They are two very different, very strong signs. Aquarius wants freedom, and Capricorn is about the rules. Her conventional approach to life frustrates the

free-spirited Aquarius. Self-expression and adventure is his motto. Stability and morality are
her strong suits. Aquarius is constantly on the
go and enjoys spending money. No attempt on
tight-fisted Capricorn's behalf to get Aquarius to
change will work.

Even on the subject of sex, they clash. Sex
for Capricorn is a way of expressing emotion or
bonding with her mate. For the Aquarius, well,
it's just sex. When she wants to express her love
for him with a night of passion, he might be off
consoling a friend or another lover. Capricorn
believes life begins when you commit to another
person. Aquarius holds tight to his conviction
that variety is the spice of life, and sex is not
excluded. It's unlikely he'll ever commit to a
Capricorn.

At best, this is a short romp in the bed.

Aquarius Man/Aquarius Woman

Finally, we have a relationship that makes
sense. This combination is the most compatible
of all the pairs. These two are destined to become
best friends and the best of lovers. These are two
intelligent people who want to affect change in
the world. They are usually involved in many
outside activities and projects and can go days

without spending time together, which is never a problem.

Sexually, they are mentally aroused before anything physical ever takes place. Sex does not need to play a major role in their relationship, but they will take care of each other's needs. Foreplay is not a necessity, and sex might last for an afternoon, or it could last as long as it takes one or both of them to reach his or her fifth orgasm. Spontaneous and free describes these two.

As business partners, they are a good match. But first, they will have to agree on who is going to be the boss. This is challenging, because with these two intellects, it can be difficult to abide by the other's decisions. It may make for a bruised ego.

Outside of business, they haven't a thing to fight about. Their love may not be rooted in heartfelt deep emotion, but it is true, and they have a definite chance at a long-lasting relationship.

Aquarius Man/Pisces Woman

Pisces is an ideal lover for Aquarius. She is quite surprised by this, because outside of the bedroom, it is hard to believe they are from the same planet. There's lots of steamy sex with these two, so hang the DO NOT DISTURB sign on the door, 'cause there will be hours upon hours of hot, sexy fun.

Aquarius and Pisces are both highly intuitive people. If they never utter a word, each will still know exactly what body part the other person wants caressed. The Pisces woman helps the Aquarius man get in touch with his emotions, and he will help her detach a bit from hers. If he's smart, he will never take Pisces's need to please as a weakness.

Outside the bedroom, Pisces is likely to grow tired of Aquarius's flighty, eccentric behavior. She will immediately move from sex partners to a sex-less friendship. The only way a long-term relationship will come out of this is if both make some serious personality adjustments. Let's just have fun and call it a day.

Famous Aquarius Men

JANUARY 20–FEBRUARY 18

Michael Jordan—February 17, 1963
Chris Rock—February 7, 1966
Jackie Robinson—January 31, 1919
Sam Cooke—January 22, 1931
Lionel Richie—January 29, 1949
Bobby Brown—February 5, 1969
Arsenio Hall—February 12, 1955
Gregory Hines—February 14, 1946
Robert Townsend—February 6, 1957
Langston Hughes—February 1, 1902

Pisces

February 19–March 20

Your Pisces Man

If you meet a man who listens to all your dreams and desires, no matter how unrealistic, and makes you believe they are possible, then chances are you have met a Pisces man. He is the romantic of the zodiac, and he loves to be in love.

Pisces spends his life dreaming of that perfect partner who will fulfill his deepest needs, and he doesn't take the search for his princess lightly. He will spend as much time as possible with a woman, trying her on like a glass slipper, to see if she fits. If a woman wants a Pisces man, she must be willing to let her life become an open book. Before long, she might feel like she's interviewing for a job she's no longer sure she wants. After all, this brother has not even tried to take her into the bedroom.

If you think for one moment that the Pisces's hesitancy about sex is because of his bedroom skills, you are in for a surprise. This is a brother who holds it down in the bedroom. He is so certain about his skills that he doesn't feel the need to prove anything by bedding a bunch of women. He has too much respect for women to limit their place in his life to the bedroom. Most Pisces are extremely close to their mothers, and they see all women as an extension of her. If there is one thing Pisces will never do, it's disrespect his mom.

Speaking of mothers, sometimes a Pisces's mate will feel like she has to be his parent. Pisces was born with rose colored glasses and usually sees the world as this beautiful, loving place where all his dreams are met. He needs to be with someone who will help him remove the glasses and see life from another point of view. For instance, show him the more sensible way to reach his dreams: work, work and work. He has lots of dreams, but sometimes lacks the ability to move in a direction to make them come true. He does need a little push, and if it's later in life for him, he'll need a big heave-ho to get off the couch and find his passion in order to make his dreams come true.

Be careful not to push a Pisces man too hard, though. The super-sensitive Pisces has a fragile heart, and remembers every mean or insensitive thing he's ever experienced since birth. Don't be surprised when he tells you a story of a friend who hurt his feelings, and he's as upset as if it happened yesterday. Before you get indignant and want to berate this friend, ask him exactly when this event occurred. You might be surprised to find out that the slight occurred in grade school. Pisces can revisit every hurt both physically and emotionally. It's not that he's not tough; he simply feels everything deeply.

He also feels deeply about the people in his life. If you're in a crisis and you need someone to have your back, Pisces is capable of superhuman strength during these moments. He has the ability to rise up and take care of everyone. Pisces hates to see anyone in trouble because he is incapable of hurting a fly. He is the bleeding heart, rescuing wounded animals and taking care of the elderly type. To him, the world would be a better place if we all did our share, so he'll be quick to lend a hand to those in need.

It's important to the Pisces that his work has the ability to transform the lives of those less fortunate. So whatever he chooses to do for a living, it will have to feed his need to be of service to the world. He is not selfish; instead, he focuses much of his time on others, sometimes to the point of unhealthiness. He is a spiritual being who needs to feel connected to his higher power.

Sometimes this means he'll choose his profession even if it doesn't pay well. Now, if you're into your Pisces, then we have to talk about money. Pisces really believes that money grows on trees. If you have money, then it means it can be spent on a whim. Pisces is not good at saving money. He likes to enjoy life and to live well.

Pisces is usually dressed from head to toe. This is a brother who likes to look his best and won't step out of the house unless he is done to death. He takes pride in how he looks, and expects you to also. He won't be flashy or loud in dress or manner. Think of the fish, calmly swimming in beautiful blue waters, and you'll know exactly who this gentleman is. And he's willing to spend good money to always present that appearance.

Unless you have fat pockets, don't let this man be in charge of the finances. He'll be on his way to pay the light bill when something beautiful catches his eye, and well, you'll be eating by candlelight—which, he'll remind you, is much more romantic anyway. Pisces has the ability to make the most of a bad situation, no matter who made it that way. Don't bother to read him about his careless attitude about money. He won't hear anything he doesn't want to hear. And if you repeat it time and time again, he'll act like he has amnesia.

Now, if the financial difficulty happens to be caused by you, don't worry. He won't flinch. Pisces will double up on his jobs to make sure you have what you need. He is forgiving of his mate's mistakes, and will always try to take care of her in her times of need.

In return, the Pisces needs to be treated like Prince Charming. But most women don't mind doing this for their Pisces men, because it's not a one way street. He'll raise his woman up on a pedestal too.

When he's not with his special woman, Pisces likes to spend plenty of time alone. Most Pisces are highly creative and artistic, and need time to think, away from others. Pisces spends lots of time forming a deeper spiritual relationship in order to feel one with the world. He believes he is in this life for a reason and has a real purpose, which is one of the reasons he needs a lot of down time to reflect. Because of this, some people will accuse the Pisces of being aloof.

This is not the case, though. Pisces is just a deep thinker who appreciates his privacy and the comfort of his own home.

This doesn't mean that he will never socialize. In fact, Pisces has the ability to take on the moods and feelings of those around him. If it's festive, then he's the life of the party, but if the mood is somber, he will be the most compassionate, thoughtful friend in the room. Because he's so deep and can change so quickly, it can be hard to pin down the true Pisces nature.

If you can deal with his sensitivity and his tendency to get lost in his dreams, the Pisces man will be a good match for you. He'll do whatever it takes to win your heart, and for a while, you'll feel like you're a princess in a fairytale.

Let's Get It Started

Pisces is a water sign, and all three water signs are extremely romantic. The fish is the dreamer of the zodiac, and he wants his partner to be one too. It's okay if you're generally a practical person, but if you can't relax from time to time to indulge in your imaginative side, then you won't do well with a Pisces.

You'll find a Pisces by looking into the center of a crowd of female admirers, gathered around, waiting for the witty conversation to fall out of his mouth. It's not hard to recognize that he's different from most guys. He actually seems to be giving something important to these women: validation. He seems genuinely interested in what they have to say, and supportive of their ideas.

There are plenty of ways to draw the Pisces's attention toward you. Mention theater, music or painting and watch how quickly he responds. He is a creative individual, and is interested in artistic things that reflect a person's soul. The Pisces is also open to many new ideas. He won't laugh if you tell him that you believe you were someone famous in a past life. In fact, he might decide to share his own theories on reincarnation with you. If you know something about dream therapy, the Fish will be hooked. You'll be happy to see some of the more skeptical sisters leaving the circle once you start interpreting his dreams for him. Before you know it, it'll be just you and your Pisces man making plans to spend more time together.

When it comes to your first date, make sure you look good when he picks you up. Pisces might be a deep thinker, but he can be shallow when it comes to appearance. He spends lots of time making sure he's on point before he steps out in public, and he'll want his woman to do the same. Pick something that is feminine and flirty, and even if you don't have a perfect ten figure, he will be attracted to you if you exude confidence. Pisces wants someone who is comfortable in her own skin.

Appeal to the Pisces's artistic side by inviting him to a performance where he might be asked to participate, or take him to karaoke and watch him blow the audience away with his talent. You might also want to take him dancing, since the Fish loves to move. His body responds to rhythms, and when he gets lost in the music, you'll wish it were you.

When it's time to eat, choose a restaurant with romantic atmosphere. Soft music and candlelit tables will impress him much more than a loud, crowded theme restaurant. He'll appreciate a quiet corner table where the two of you can chat and get to know each other better. Well, actually, he'll let you do most of the talking. He's a great listener, because he's trying to learn all he can about a woman to see if she is his type. Do him a favor and don't make him prod you for answers about yourself. If you have to, offer him a list of ref-erences—friends and family who can vouch for you. He'll appreciate the humor.

He'll like to know that you share some common interests, so once you figure out what those are, focus on them. But be sure he understands that if you become a couple, you won't expect more togetherness than he can handle. He doesn't want the heavy responsibility that comes from being anybody's sole focus. To have a shot at this man, you must show him just how well rounded and independent you can be. Having your own life will add major points to your overall score with Pisces.

After a night of deep conversation and perhaps some sexy moves on the dance floor, you might expect some immediate feedback from the Pisces about your chances with him. Don't be too disappointed if you don't get it right away. The Pisces isn't known to jump into the sack too soon, no matter how well the date went or how much he likes you. He believes in romance, and wants all the elements to be perfect before he takes that next step. Your best bet is to give him plenty of compliments to let him know what a good impression he's made on you. Thank him for being so respectful, and tell him you hope you can see him again soon. Have some patience, and keep an upbeat attitude as you wait for the Pisces to make his next move. When he finally does, you will be well rewarded with all his attention and his affection.

Keeping Him Happy

- Hire a psychic to give him a reading.
- Read poetry in front of a fire.
- Give him lots of compliments.
- Don't complain about his tendency to daydream.
- Never nag him about anything.
- Pretend it's Valentine's Day all the time.
- Download romantic music onto his iPod.
- Feed him sexy desserts, like chocolate cake.
- Take him to the theater.
- Surprise him with a picnic on the beach.

Sex

The time for a Pisces man to have sex is now. Whenever and wherever he wants to have sex, you better be ready. He doesn't have a lot of patience for playing games and being kept waiting. If this is the man you want, I suggest you go with the program. And by the way, it will always be his program. That's not to say you won't enjoy it, but when he decides to have sex, he really needs it right then and there.

Although he is a romantic when it comes to the other areas of his life, Pisces can be a bit of a freak in the bedroom. Outside the bedroom he's a dreamer, but in bed, he is interested in exploring every one of his sexual fantasies.

Pisces like to add an extra thrill element, which sometimes leads to his interest in married women. Oh, the drama of being with an unavailable woman heightens his sexual pleasure. He is not interested in virginal women. The Fish likes to be with an experienced woman who doesn't mind taking the lead and undressing him. If she has a little bit of the dominatrix in her, so much the better, because chances are he's been a very bad boy.

Because the Pisces is a water sign, anything that includes water is erotic to him. Showers, Jacuzzis and pools are places where he likes to explore sexual satisfaction. His favorite activities involve the feet, so keep your pedicure current because you'll be using those feet in the bedroom. He'll want you to take his penis between your toes and massage him to orgasm. And if you're trying to keep him turned on, always wear the sexiest shoes you can find.

If you've just begun a relationship with the Pisces, you may not have any clue what I'm talking about, but give him time. The closer he gets to you, the more he'll let you experience his wild side. But if you want some freaky sex out of him in the beginning of a relationship, just let him know. It's impossible to make your Pisces man jealous. He believes it's important to be yourself, and he's open minded about whatever that includes. He is all about pleasing his partner, even if that means watching her masturbate or have sex with another man. He'll do anything to please the woman in bed, and no matter how far from "normal" you take your fantasies, you'll always feel his complete interest and attraction to you.

If you're lucky enough to be anywhere near a bed with a Pisces man, then I suggest you go for it—and quickly, because he doesn't like to be kept waiting.

Pisces Turn-Ons

- Give him a foot massage and suck on his toes.
- Have sex in hot tubs, bathtubs, waterbeds.
- Enjoy lots of foreplay.
- Massage his penis between your toes.
- Win his trust.
- Light and playful S&M.
- Share your fantasies with him.
- Be ready for sex whenever he is.
- Perform a striptease.

Moving On Without Drama

If you have gotten a Pisces man to fall for you, then you are going to have some problems letting go because the Fish will stick to you like glue. He tends to hold such a romanticized view of love that no matter how bad a woman is for him, he will hold on to the fantasy that she is his perfect woman.

I know three different women who cheated on their Pisces mates. Even after the affairs came to light, not one of these Pisces wanted the relationship to end, and all the couples stayed together. This is how I know for sure that it is hard to leave a Pisces man. He isn't considered one of the most charming men in the zodiac for no reason. He knows how to change your mind by reminding you what a great catch he is.

So, if you've had the talk and still can't seem to get this brother to say bye-bye, here are some ways to get him to go. Just be prepared to deal with the guilt because if he leaves, you'll know you've hurt him deeply. I've already told you how Pisces is about remembering every emotional wound he's ever received. You'll be forever remembered as the woman who broke his heart.

Pisces can live solely on compliments. In fact, he needs the flattery just about as much as he needs fresh air. So naturally, you must become very critical of your Pisces man. Tell him he has no sense of style and you're sick of everything in his wardrobe. He'll offer to change to please you, but tell him you've closed the checking account because of his spending habits, and you won't give him any money to buy new clothes. From that point on, he'll feel self conscious every time he sees you looking disdainfully at whatever he's wearing.

Now you've wounded his feelings, and he'll be feeling pretty insecure around you. As cold as it sounds, this is when you move in for the kill and finish off his ego. Remember, your Pisces man respects you completely, so give him reasons to doubt his own opinion of you. Practice poor hygiene, and laugh too loud at crass jokes. When your Pisces whines about some slight that happened to him, just tell him to get over it and stop being such a baby. Your days of being his "Mommy" are over. When he tries to share his feelings or his dreams with you, tell him you're tired of hearing his daydreaming nonsense. Tell him it's time to get off his behind and find a real job.

No matter how much you've hurt him, your Pisces will stick with you if your sexual relationship is still alive. So no matter how good the sex is, you must refuse to go to bed with him. This will be the final straw, and even the ever-faithful Pisces will decide it's time to call it quits.

Just remember this: Before you do all these things, make sure you're ready to give him up because he won't be available for casual sex once you've broken his heart.

Compatibility

PISCES

Pisces Man/Aries Woman

These two work well together, but only in the bedroom. Pisces brings the sexual energy, while Aries has the take charge personality. Aries will take the lead, and Pisces doesn't have a problem with it. He enjoys low-down, nasty sex, and she will go right there with him, if only to prove that she's incredible. Aries might also have a few moves Pisces has never seen before. They are the perfect 69 couple, who love to get and won't mind giving in return.

Aries can be controlling and likes to be a party girl. Pisces is easy and prefers to stay at home. He needs his privacy and wants time to be alone and reflect. The problem is that Aries needs lots of attention and admiration, and won't have much patience for his dreamy inattention.

This is definitely not a love connection.

Pisces Man/Taurus Woman

Pisces can enjoy sex in many positions and in many places. Foreplay can start just by a sensual hand holding episode.

Taurus will enjoy watching her man in this state, and actually find herself feeling stimulated as well. Sex should be kept simple; romance just the same. Don't forget masturbation, Pisces. She will be happy to watch and will definitely assist.

Sex is not going to be the downfall of this duo. Money, however, is at the top of the list of possible problems. Taurus might want to pay attention to the finances. Even though the Taurus likes to spend money, she also likes to earn it, while the Pisces doesn't have a problem spending it, even if he's not earning it. Pisces will forget to pay the bills and Taurus might find herself making love in the dark, but not by choice. She shouldn't "show him the money" if she knows what's good for the relationship.

If they can get their financial differences under control, this couple can be together for as long as they desire. This would be a fun wedding.

Pisces Man/Gemini Woman

It will take too much to make this duo work. The sex is not hot at all, because their rhythms are so different. Just as Pisces gets used to Gemini and her wild sexual ideas, she has moved on to something else. Perhaps it's her evil twin that's causing all the confusion. Pisces is too emotional and needy for the indifferent Gemini.

The twins like to have total freedom, but the Pisces needs reassurances that his Gemini woman loves and appreciates him. These two may never understand each other, but if each could just let the other be, they might have a chance for something decadent and temporary. This is one of those couples who you watch just because you're waiting for the wheels to come off of the relationship.

Pisces Man/Cancer Woman

Pisces and Cancer are both sensual individuals who are intuitive and artistic. These two are referred to as the soul mates of the zodiac. There is strong spiritual and sexual chemistry.

Although these signs are different in some ways, it doesn't outweigh all the good things about them as a couple. Cancer is great with money and forgives Pisces's messy bank account. Both are deeply emotional and feeling individuals, who are in touch with their inner feelings. Both are better in long-term relationships instead of one-night stands. They are physically attuned, in and out of the bedroom. A good after-sexual activity is to settle into one another's arms and stay there until there's a need to go elsewhere.

As water signs, these two live to go deep, so they both feel excited to have found each other. This is more than a marriage. They are soul mates.

Pisces Man/Leo Woman

Pisces might have a hard time with the extrovert Leo as his mate, but sexually, they can have fun. Leo likes to take control, while the Pisces loves to be controlled. He likes the dominatrix side of the Lion and submits to his mistress. As freaky as Pisces can be, he still might find himself needing a drink or two to help him relax and let go to keep up with the Leo.

Pisces is sensitive and Leo feels protective of whomever makes her feel safe. But eventually, his overly emotional nature might turn her off. She wants a man's man, and the Pisces is too sensitive to be as manly as she needs.

Skip this one and go to the movies.

Pisces Man/Virgo Woman

These two easygoing people will do well once they make a connection. Although their signs are opposite, sex can be amazing. Kissing, caressing, and tickling are all great ways to get them going. Neither one minds if the other one is in control. They will roll over many times, allowing each one the opportunity to enjoy sex from the top. Pisces will let loose in the bedroom. His goal is to please his Virgo woman and break her shell. Virgo should be prepared for lots of deep, emotional conversations both in and out of the bedroom.

Between the two of them, Virgo is the practical one. Pisces is a dreamer, while Virgo is the doer. This combination works better when the sexes are reversed. When Pisces is dreaming about his next great invention or business idea, there is still all the day to day practical stuff that needs to get done, and guess who will have to handle it? It's not that he doesn't want to help out, he's just not great at the practical side of life.He will gladly turn over all the things he doesn't want to do, like planning and scheduling, to Virgo. But if she tries to change him, she will only become more frustrated.

When they connect, these two do not need anyone else in their world. They are easygoing and can make for a great night all by themselves. Still, the only way anything will last is if it's a friendship.

Pisces Man/Libra Woman

This duo may last for a bit. They can expect some good sex and good times ahead.

Music, drinking, and dancing are some of the ways the duo will spend time together when not holed up behind closed doors. Now, if they are in one of their passive moods, sex may take a while to get going. But whenever lovemaking is initiated, this hot combo will definitely enjoy some passionate sex. Both are masters of foreplay, so these two will send each other to ecstasy without any penetration. There is lots of sexual juiciness between them, since Libra likes to watch and Pisces likes to perform.

They each like to talk and can spend hours on a good topic. It's easy for these two to go from a steamy sex duo to a spiritual duo. They might want to pull out the timer to keep a check on those long talks. Since both are long-winded and passionate, it's easy to get distracted, causing the needs of the relationship to take a back seat.

There is lots of passion waiting, so it's worth the effort it will take. This is so crazy it might just work.

Pisces Man/Scorpio Woman

Intense, exciting and magical are great words to describe this duo. Beware of sparks flying if you are in their presence when they first meet. Sexually, they are off the charts. It will go beyond the soul, almost mystical, stirring up emotions that neither knew was possible. They could not have found more perfect partners.

No need to watch pornography to get in the mood. Sex with this duo is erotic, exhilarating and enlivening. They are naturally drawn to each other. This just might be love at first sight.

Both complement each other and will remain loyal because understanding comes without effort. The Scorpio woman finds the Pisces's dreaming inspiring and exciting. There is still a lack of follow-through on Pisces's behalf, but with all the other pluses—great sex, great conversation, devotion— what's a little follow-through problem? There's always going to be something. Pisces's commitment to the relationship brings Scorpio comfort.

Lots of marriages have resulted from this combination.

Pisces Man/Sagittarius Woman

Watch out! If you're looking for a lasting love, look the other way.

The Sagittarius woman will be drawn to Pisces's alluring sexual aura, but remember, relationships are built on more than multiple orgasms. Sex will be good, but love is another story. Pisces is too emotional for Sagittarius's outgoing and fun personality. Pisces will mistake any support offered as a sign of a true love. But when she stops showering him with reassurance, he will feel threatened and neglected. That sexual intrigue these two had when they first met will start to dissipate overtime. Sagittarius will begin to find Pisces's approach to life draining and unrealistic, and the sexual attraction will start to dwindle.

If they can enjoy this sexual encounter for what it is, they'll have a better chance at a friendship. Expecting anything more than sex from this union will leave them both . . . alone.

Pisces Man/Capricorn Woman

If they're looking for real love, Pisces and Capricorn might want to stick this one out. The two of them will form an instant friendship that will quickly turn sexual, which is a bonus for the slow Capricorn.

Sex will vary with these two. One night will be romantic and engaging with candlelight, and the next night might be hot and earthy, with naked bodies under a self-made tent. They are both great kissers, so they should take advantage of lip action as often as possible. Kissing is a great way to start off a night of passionate sex. It will lead both to the heights of physical ecstasy.

Pisces's passionate nature works well with Capricorn's calm demeanor. Capricorn will help center him and calm his active imagination, while Pisces will show Capricorn life's variety. The Pisces man provides emotional support, and will cherish the Capricorn's loyalty.

Sounds like a keeper to me. Don't let this one get away.

Pisces Man/Aquarius Woman

If you want to take a short trip downhill fast, this is the combination for you. This relationship may seem to have all of the qualities for lasting love, but Pisces and Aquarius will shortly see how wrong they are for each other.

Initially, they form such a special bond, they mistake it for something deeper. It isn't.

Sex, on the other hand . . . well, let's just say it will never be boring. Steamy, hot, crazy, wild— that's what they'll have to look forward to between the sheets. With these two, don't rule out sex up against the wall in a public bathroom. Pisces is an ideal lover, and he will send Aquarius soaring.

But Pisces expects his woman to be open and honest, so Aquarius's manipulative ways will not work for him. Pisces has a tendency to be clingy. He will complain about Aquarius spending too much time with her inventions and volunteering. That's just who she is, and she won't even think of changing for him.

I know, the sex sounds so phenomenal that you can't imagine passing it up. They should remember, though, that it's just sex between the two of them, since anything more will fizzle and leave them wondering why they bothered in the first place.

This is a good friends-with-benefits kind of relationship.

Pisces Man/Pisces Woman

One might think that if you put two Pisces together, it would add up to a happy couple. Well, they may find happiness together in some areas, but in most areas, there is something missing.

Sex is quite good because they love to do it deeply and often. Both instinctively know what the other wants because it's usually the same thing they need. They become absorbed in their bond and find themselves caught up in their partner as well.

Nonetheless, when Pisces's emotions get in the way, they'll have trouble making a sound decision about anything. There is a lot of high and low dramas with these two. Finances will be a big problem, since neither of them knows how to save a dime. Things could be less challenging if one of them was more practical, but it's not likely to work with two dreamers swimming in different directions without a partner to reel them in once in a while.

This relationship is not a keeper.

Famous Pisces Men

FEBRUARY 19–MARCH 20

Terence Howard—March 11, 1969
Quincy Jones—March 14, 1933
Flavor Flav—March 16, 1959
Reggie Bush—March 2, 1965
Spike Lee—March 20, 1957
Timbaland—March 10, 1971
Clifton Powell—March 16, 1956
Mikylt Williamson—March 4, 1960
Sidney Poitier- February 20, 1927
Rodney Peete—March 16, 1966
D.L. Hughley—March 6, 1963
Boris Kodjoe—March 8, 1973

Notes

Notes

Notes

ORDER FORM
URBAN BOOKS, LLC
78 E. Industry Ct
Deer Park, NY 11729

Name: (please print):_____

Address:_____

City/State:_____

Zip:_____

QTY	TITLES	PRICE

Shipping and handling-add $3.50 for 1st book, then $1.75 for each additional book. Please send a check payable to:
Urban Books, LLC
Please allow 4-6 weeks for delivery

ORDER FORM
URBAN BOOKS, LLC
78 E. Industry Ct
Deer Park, NY 11729

Name: (please print): _____

Address: _____

City/State: _____

Zip: _____

QTY	TITLES	PRICE
	16 On The Block	$14.95
	A Girl From Flint	$14.95
	A Pimp's Life	$14.95
	Baltimore Chronicles	$14.95
	Baltimore Chronicles 2	$14.95
	Betrayal	$14.95
	Black Diamond	$14.95
	Black Diamond 2	$14.95
	Black Friday	$14.95
	Both Sides Of The Fence	$14.95
	Both Sides Of The Fence 2	$14.95
	California Connection	$14.95

Shipping and handling-add $3.50 for 1st book, then $1.75 for each additional book.

Please send a check payable to:

Urban Books, LLC

Please allow 4-6 weeks for delivery

ORDER FORM
URBAN BOOKS, LLC
78 E. Industry Ct
Deer Park, NY 11729

Name: (please print): _____

Address: _____

City/State: _____

Zip: _____

QTY	TITLES	PRICE
	California Connection 2	$14.95
	Cheesecake And Teardrops	$14.95
	Congratulations	$14.95
	Crazy In Love	$14.95
	Cyber Case	$14.95
	Denim Diaries	$14.95
	Diary Of A Mad First Lady	$14.95
	Diary Of A Stalker	$14.95
	Diary Of A Street Diva	$14.95
	Diary Of A Young Girl	$14.95
	Dirty Money	$14.95
	Dirty To The Grave	$14.95

Shipping and handling-add $3.50 for 1st book, then $1.75 for each additional book.
Please send a check payable to:
Urban Books, LLC
Please allow 4-6 weeks for delivery

ORDER FORM
URBAN BOOKS, LLC
78 E. Industry Ct
Deer Park, NY 11729

Name:(please print):_____

Address: _____

City/State: _____

Zip: _____

QTY	TITLES	PRICE
	Gunz And Roses	$14.95
	Happily Ever Now	$14.95
	Hell Has No Fury	$14.95
	Hush	$14.95
	If It Isn't love	$14.95
	Kiss Kiss Bang Bang	$14.95
	Last Breath	$14.95
	Little Black Girl Lost	$14.95
	Little Black Girl Lost 2	$14.95
	Little Black Girl Lost 3	$14.95
	Little Black Girl Lost 4	$14.95
	Little Black Girl Lost 5	$14.95

Shipping and handling-add $3.50 for 1st book, then $1.75 for each additional book.
Please send a check payable to:
   Urban Books, LLC
Please allow 4-6 weeks for delivery